The Book of the Roger St. Pierre
BICYCLE

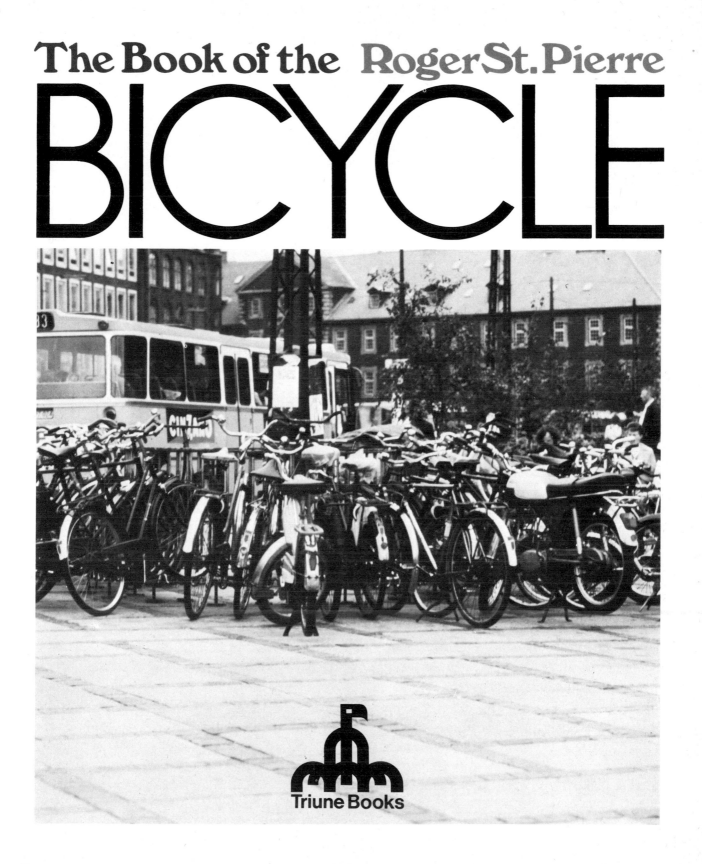

Triune Books

Acknowledgments

Photographs were supplied by the following:

Associated Press: 53*t*, 90*r*; Barnaby's Picture Library: 12*tr*, 57, 103; Bellwether: 32*t*, 32*b*; British Cycling Bureau: 20*t*, 20*b*, 33*t*, 33*b*; Camera Press: 10, 11*r*; Neville Chanin: 55, 63, 91; H. T. Comerford: 85; Conway Picture Library: jacket front *tr*, 50*b*, 88*t*, 89*tr*, 101*b*, 102*b*, 104*t*; 'Cycling': 18*t*, 18*b*, 20*t*, 22, 23, 27*t*, 28, 34*l*, 34*r*, 35, 36*b*, 45, 53*c*, 67*r*, 89*c*, 89*b*, 90*tl*, 92, 93*t*, 94*b*, 95*b*, 98*b*, 101*t*, 104*b*, 105*b*; Cyclists Touring Club: 66, 81*r*; C. C. P. Davies: 82, 83*t*, 86*tl*, 86*tr*, 87*t*; E. Dayer: 58; Dave Dieter: 79*b*; Peter Duker: 84*b*; Robert Estall: 72*t*, 72*bl*, 72*br*, 73*t*, 73*b*, 77; Mary Evans Picture Library: 38–39, 40*l*, 41*r*, 44, 47*t*, 54; Friends of Bikecology, Santa Barbara, California: 14; International Bicycle Touring Society: 52*t*, 53, 85*t*, 86*b*; Keystone Press Agency: 110; Bill Leimbach: 62*b*, 79, 83*t*, 85*b*; F. W. Loasby: 78; Geoffrey Magnay: 15*tr*, 15*tl*, 36*t*, 90*b*, 93*b*, 94*t*, 96*t*, 96*b*, 97, 100*t*, 100*b*; Mansell Collection: 42*t*, 43*l*; Opel: 46*b*; Axel Poignant: 13; Barry Pringle: 12*tl*, 68; Radio Times Hulton Picture Library: 37, 40–41, 42*b*, 44*r*, 46*t*, 47*b*, 52*c*; Raleigh Industries Ltd: 18, 53*b*; Rally Enterprises: 17*t*; Slide Centre: 51; Spectrum Colour Library: jacket front *l*, *b*; 12*bl*, 12*br*, 16, 50*t*, 59, 61, 62*t*, 65, 69, 95*t*, 98*tl*, 98*tr*, 102; P. T. Stallard: 49; Syndication International: 52*b*; Bernard Thompson: 67*l*, 87*b*; Topix: 60; Transworld Features: 11*l*; U.P.I.: 8.

The publishers gratefully acknowledge the loan by Condor Cycles of equipment for the photographs on pages 72 and 73, and the facilities provided by Hetchin's, London N15, for the photography of decorative lugwork (front endpapers)

Diagrams drawn by Ken Lewis

ISBN 0 85674 010 1
Published by
Triune Books. London, England
© Trewin Copplestone Publishing Ltd 1973
Printed in Spain
by Printer industria gráfica sa Tuset, 19 Barcelona
San Vicente dels Horts 1973
Depósito legal B. 17108-1973
Mohn Gordon Ltd. London

Contents

Bicycling: the pathway to fitness...

. . . and fun

Other sports have their attractions, but none has such diverse appeal as cycling. After all, you cannot very well kick a football to work, or spend your holidays touring the country on ice-skates.

The scope of cycling ranges from sporting competitions to organised touring, from simple sightseeing to everyday utility work between home and work-place. It combines the speed elements of motorised sports with the health-giving aspects of physcial sports and athletics. The simple bicycle is a cheap and efficient means of transport. It is also a source of enjoyment. There is something particularly gratifying about getting around under your own steam and, with rides of a hundred miles and more well within the capabilities of the reasonably fit rider from sub-teens to senior-citizens, there is the pleasure of change of scene and discovery at minimal expense.

Engaging almost every muscle of the body in some degree, cycling has health-giving attributes. Cyclists are noted for their development of strong hearts and lusty lungs. Health

Many show business people, David Cassidy included, find bicycling an ideal recreation. Brigitte Bardot, Eric Clapton, Jackie Onassis and Mayor Lindsay of New York are other bicycling celebrities

The 'mini-bike' small-wheeler revolution brought a new respectability to the humble bicycle. Even the British Lord Chancellor, Lord Hailsham, finds it ideal for daily rounds between affairs of state

experts—both practising doctors and laymen—generally agree that few forms of exercise are as good for health as cycling. Unlike exercises in the gym, it is not boring: seeking fitness, you can rediscover the countryside, visit places of interest or go shopping!

It is no longer 'infra dig' to ride a bike. City businessmen, High Court Judges, US senators, health-fiends and ecology campaigners all extol its merits. Sales of cycles are now at an all-time high in America and show no signs of abating, while other countries are also experiencing a revival. So much so that there is a severe world shortage of new bikes and replacement parts, the factories being unable to keep pace with demand. This, and increasing interest of the Japanese in both competitive and pleasure bicycling, has led Japanese industries to invest heavily in new factories for bicycles and their accessories. They are now taking a large share of the world market.

The sporting side is winning new converts, and for once it is as participants rather than spectators that they are being attracted—a

As beast-of-burden, commuter transport, child-carrier,
even as a 'home-on-wheels' for the lonely swagman,
the bicycle is a trusty and long-serving friend

healthy trend in a world where too many people are content to watch the sporting activities of others on the television screens.

As roads become clogged with motor traffic and standards of public transport decline, people are increasingly turning to the bicycle as the sensible answer, and the legislators have not been slow to appreciate its worth. In this respect, the USA undoubtedly leads the world. Although Holland and Denmark—countries in which the bicycle has always retained its popularity—have long provided facilities for its use, these have consisted simply of rather narrow pathways alongside motor roads, and are often blocked by parked cars and other obstructions. But in America there are now several thousand miles of special bike-routes. Many are far removed from any motor roads, taking riders through some of the most beautiful scenery that vast and varied land has to offer, while others protect cyclists by running special 'bike only' lanes through busy city and suburban streets.

Many notable concessions have been granted to American cyclists. For instance, the roads of New York's Central Park are reserved for cyclists on certain days of the week, and many

Specially-designed bicycle paths are becoming a feature of road programmes in many countries. Compare the bicyclists' ease of progress with all those queueing motor vehicles!

thousands of wheelmen—and wheel-women and children too—take the chance to enjoy a few hours pleasant riding away from any danger of accidents with motor vehicles. Mayor John B. Lindsay has been an important figure in establishing the cyclist's role in his city and is himself an enthusiastic rider.

In Britain, too, cycling now has its foothold in Parliament with a 'Friends of Cycling' group of MPs looking after its interests. Special 'bus-only' lanes in busy city streets are now being opened to cyclists as well. The town of Stevenage boasts an extensive and much-used cycleway system, and many miles of bridlepath, disused rail routes and remote mountain track in Britain are now being opened to cyclists.

The bicycle has a real function to fulfil in modern society. Unlike the invention of the internal combustion engine, this simple yet efficient means of personal transportation has conferred infinite good and very few problems on the world since it was developed from a child's plaything to a finely-engineered peice of craftmanship which has given mobility and enjoyment to millions of people around the world.

15

Buying a bicycle

Far too many people dismiss cycling off-hand as being 'too much like hard work'. Looking at the kind of machines on which they have done their pedalling, it is easy to see why they have come to that conclusion. There is a world of truth in the axiom that you have got to have the right tools for the job, and this applies as much to cycling as to anything else.

A bewildering choice of cycles greets the potential customer at any cycle store and, unfortunately, too many dealers are too anxious to make a quick sale, neglecting their duty to ensure that the correct type of machine is offered. Most cycles manufactured today are admirable, provided they are used for the job they have been designed to handle. The best racing machine in the world will be next to useless as a bike for daily shopping-trips; the finest touring machine would never do for a road race; and a utility mount designed for short trips around town is bound to make legs ache on a long ride through hilly country. So, before buying a bike, it is important to consider exactly what functions you want it to fulfil. Those who take their cycling really seriously think nothing of owning half-a-dozen or more bikes, each kitted out differently to fill a specific role.

For racing alone, more than one machine is needed if you want to take part in all types of event. Road-racing demands a multi-geared machine, fitted with two reliable brakes; a single-geared, fixed-wheel bike with no brakes is mandatory for track racing, while a specially adapted bike with wide wheel clearances and special 'knobbly' tubular tyres will be required for cyclo-cross (cross-country) events.

Let us examine the main types of bicycle generally available in cycle shops around the world. As complete machines, six basic models are on offer, though there is considerable overlap between the various types, and great variety within each classification.

The bicycle store is a long-established feature of towns and villages around the world

1. The heavy roadster machine, fitted with roller brakes, wide-section tyres, steel rims and a chain totally encased in an oil-filled gear-case. Thankfully, this cumbersome monstrosity is going out of fashion, though it does still find a certain market in Africa and the Far East, especially as a beast of burden.

2. The sports roadster, known in the United States as the English racer, though it could not be found in any race I have ever seen. This is a lighter, far more responsive version of the roadster, fitted with cable brakes, comfortable 'flat' handlebars, mudguards and, as often as not, three, four or five-speed derailleur gearing. With the addition of pannier carriers for transport of luggage, this is an ideal mount for shopping and work trips.

3. The club sports or semi-racer. Fitted with dropped handlebars, 5–15 speed derailleur gearing, alloy rims and light high-pressure tyres, this is the kind of machine which is becoming increasingly popular in the States. With small modifications (such as the addition of mudguards, saddlebag or panniers) it is ideal for touring work and, at a pinch, can be converted into a racing machine through the substitution of tubular racing tyres and 'sprint' rims.

4. The true lightweight, road racing bike. A hand-made frame, built from double-butted section tubing (wider in internal gauge at the tube ends, giving increased strength while saving on weight compared with conventional 'plain-gauge' tubing), it is the ultimate in sophistication, employing 10 to 15 gears, cotterless chainset, all-alloy accessories and ultra-light wheels with tubular tyres. The same basic machine is used by experienced tourists—they simply substitute heavier wheels and tyres, wider-range gearing, add pannier carriers and mudguards, and fit handlebars with a slightly shallower drop.

5. The track-racing or path model. The lightest bikes of all, these have frames built to the same standards as road-racing bikes, but are fitted with rear-opening drop-outs for the back-wheel, close wheel-clearances and ultra-short wheelbase. These bikes are equipped with a single-speed fixed-wheel and are devoid of all appendages such as brakes, mudguards, gears etc. The weight of such a bike can be as little as 16 lbs and on the better tracks tyres as light as three ounces are frequently used in the quest for higher speed.

6. The small-wheeler. The introduction of the 12–18-inch-wheeler, with features like a folding frame or easily collapsible handlebar and seat assemblies, in the early 1960s was perhaps more responsible than anything else for the resurgence of cycling as a popular pursuit. Here was a machine which could be conveniently carried in a car, stowed away in the cupboard under the stairs after use and had the added advantage of ease of mounting, with one model suitable for both men and women. What is more, most bikes of this type have sufficient saddle and handlebar adjustment to make one machine suitable for everyone in the family from dad down to the ten-year-olds.

Used for shopping and work trips and for the occasional short jaunt in the country, small-wheelers are just fine, but, though some tourists swear by small-wheelers, and they have been used with some success in racing, they will never replace the conventional 27-inch-wheeled lightweights for more serious pursuits. The races they won were carefully chosen to suit the small-wheeler's particular handling characteristics. While it is certainly nippy on flat roads and is very manoeuvrable in traffic, it is a tricky customer to handle when climbing hills out of the saddle, it lacks the fine and precise steering control needed for high-speed descents and all-out finishing sprints.

Certainly the small-wheeler has a role to play as a utility machine, but it will remain something of a plaything rather than a bike for the true enthusiast. Among the small-wheelers, the Moulton developed by Alex Moulton (also responsible for the revolutionary suspension set-up on the BMC Mini automobiles) is probably the best, with the added advantage of a sprung front suspension for greater comfort. Raleigh and Peugeot also produce 'minis', and there are foldaway models, though the rigidity of their frames may be reduced as a result.

With its *derailleur* gears, flat bars and handy carrier, the
sports roadster is ideal for the casual bicyclist

Heavy but solidly made, the old-fashioned roadster
guarantees years of useful life, but also encourages the
myth that cycling has to be hard work

Adapted from racing machines, sports bikes such as
this are immensely popular with American bicyclists

Full-blown road racing machines offer the ultimate in
craftsmanship and responsiveness and can be readily
adapted for more leisurely uses

Bicycles can take many specialised forms. This machine with its small front wheel enables its rider to get closer to the motorcycle pacer in spectacular paced races, where speeds in excess of 60 mph are achieved

The invention of the small-wheeled Moulton, demonstrated **right** by former racing driver Stirling Moss, sparked a great utility cycling boom and

spawned dozens of similar machines such as the Dawes **left**

These, then, are the basic types of bike available and, for those whose interest in cycling goes beyond making local utility trips, we can discard the 'roadster', 'sports roadster' and, in the main the 'small-wheeler'. Among the 'club sports' or 'semi-racers', such makes as Peugeot, Gitane and Motobecane (French), Carlton, Sun, Coventry-Eagle and Falcon (British), Fuji and Nishiki (Japanese), Atala, Frejus, Cinelli and Bianchi (Italy) Mondia (Swiss), Windsor (Mexican) and Paramount and Schwinn (American) all have good reputations for turning out well-designed and reasonably-priced machines in this category.

Most of these factories also turn out hand-made racing bikes, replicas of those used by their professional racing teams, but enthusiasts usually prefer a 'made-to-measure' machine from one of the smaller specialist builders, as this enables them to buy a machine for their own personal requirements. There are several hundred such makers to choose from, the best operating in England and Italy, with Condor, Hetchins, Holdsworth, Bird, Jack Taylor, Mercian, Bob Jackson, Ron Cooper (all British), Colnago and Masi (Italian) among the names that spring readily to mind. From Belgium, the Plume Vainqueur, Dossche Sport and Plume Sport marques have a strong following. France's René Herse is a true thoroughbred, and Holland offers the Rih-Sport among its better marques.

Having a bike constructed to one's own specification makes a lot of sense. It is just like buying a suit: off-the-peg may be more convenient, but if your build departs at all from what is reckoned to be that of Mr Average then you are in trouble. If possible, it is always advisable to have a bike put together to one's own specification and that applies as much to choice of accessories as to frame size and style. After all, what use are mudguards to someone living in an area of minimal rainfall or wide-ratio gears to someone whose cycling will be done in an area where the steepest climb is a railway-bridge?

Should it be impossible for you to obtain a made-to-measure frame on which to hang your chosen accessories, then I would advise the purchase of a top-of-the-range road-racing frame from one of the makers already mentioned,

or some other specialist, even though racing may be the furthest thing from your mind. The extra responsiveness and careful construction of such a frame will pay dividends.

Look for Columbus, Vitus or Reynolds 531 double-butted tubing. A frame made of these should carry a transfer which says so. Beware, however, for Reynolds also make other, cheaper tubing; so look out carefully for the words 'double-butted frame-tubes and forks'.

The lively feel of such a mount will give greatly increased pleasure. It is somewhat akin to the difference between driving a Ferrari and a Ford; even if you have no interest in exploiting the full speed potential, there is a special delight in having a refined, hand-crafted machine at your disposal. In the choice of accessories you can change it from being a full-blown racer to a bike for more leisurely pleasure cycling, just as a racing Ferrari can be de-tuned for street use.

Racing or not, the use of dropped handlebars and 'rat-trap' racing pedals, fitted with toe-clips and easily-released toestraps, will both increase your cycling efficiency and your subsequent enjoyment. Moreover, they will also prove more comfortable once you have become used to them.

Dropped handlebars enable you both to cut down wind-resistance and make better use of your muscle power, since back and stomach muscles are also brought into use to aid the efforts expended through legs and arms. Moreover, provided it is not taken to stupid extremes, the crouched riding position is in the long run the most comfortable as well as the speediest, especially since dropped bars enable it to be constantly modified—you can relax on the tops when the going is easy, or drop down onto the hooks into a nagging headwind or when seeking extra speed.

Toe-clips increase efficiency enormously, enabling you to 'claw' the pedal round as well as just pushing down on it. They also prevent the danger of your feet slipping off the pedal under effort, this safety factor far outweighing the danger of toppling-over through being unable to get your feet out in time when coming to a rapid emergency stop. In any case, once the art is mastered, feet can be whipped out of the clips in a split second, even when shoe-plates (a further aid to pedalling efficiency) are also used. These are metal or rubber plates affixed to the sole of the shoe and having a groove into which the pedal plate slots, ensuring a firm connection between foot and pedal and thus an efficient drive.

Let us now examine the components which go into the construction of the modern light-weight bicycle:

Frame

Current fashion dictates a more 'upright' frame than was previously the case, the angle of the seat and head tubes having been steepened to around 72–73 degrees. The nearer the head-tube is to the vertical, the lighter the steering, resulting in a more responsive bike with finer balance—a great boon and one that can be enjoyed now that road surfaces are greatly improved.

At the same time, by steepening the seat tube, the saddle is brought further in front of the rear-wheel's centre-line, thus increasing comfort. Steeper fork-rakes and shorter wheelbases, both made feasible by today's better roads, add further to the modern machine's liveliness.

Thankfully, frame breakages are now ex-tremely rare in ordinary use, and usually occur only as the result of a violent collision. It is, however, advisable to check the standard of finish where the frame tubes have been brazed into the joining lugs. This is where trouble can occur if the joint has been carelessly made, either out of square, by overheating (which leaves burn marks and signs of bubbling, and means the tubes have been robbed of tensile strength), or by skimping on brazing fluid (meaning an incomplete joint, gaps being visible around the lugs).

There has been a great vogue for fancy lug patterns and it must be said that this can en-hance the appearance of the machine (though carried to the extreme it ends up in a frame which resembles a wrought-iron gate). Most expert cyclists prefer the simple, uncluttered lines of the popular French and Italian 'block' lugs. These make for ease of frame-building, too.

It was once held that brazed-on fittings (gear-lever bosses, cable-eyes and such like) led to weakened frame tubes, but the advent of low-temperature brazing processes removed such dangers. Today's preference for clip-on acces-sories can be put down simply to fashion, though it is a hard one to understand, when brazed on fittings not only make for neater looks but also mean things are less likely to come adrift.

A good lightweight frame can tip the scales at as little as 4 pounds, and there is a current fad for saving even more ounces through cutting chunks out of bottom-bracket lugs, head-tubes and so on. Similarly, such accessories as seat-pillars, gears, brake-levers and so on are drilled away until barely a skeleton remains. Though this practice is employed by many top European racing men, it is one which should only be carried out by expert mechanics and then with extreme caution. Lightness may in itself be a desirable quality, but not when it is gained at the

In the quest for ever-lighter racing machines, a fad for drilling away excess metal has passed beyond practical considerations into the realm of sheer fashion

expense of rigidity, reliability and safety. What is more, many of these savings in weight (mostly minute) must be offset by increased wind-resistance through turbulence set up by all those holes.

Welded frames were at one time much in vogue, offering a cleaner look as well as a saving in weight but, lacking rigidity, they have not really caught on in a big way. During the 1930s, Carminargent and other makers developed frames which utilised light alloys instead of steel tubing. One French firm even produced a fully-equipped touring machine complete with dynamo lighting, mudguards and carrier which only weighed 17 pounds all in.

Apart from their lightness and resistance to corrosion, alloy frames had the added advantage that they could be literally dyed (anodised) in the desired colour, thus giving a completely unchippable finish. Once again, it was the same bugbear of insufficient rigidity which prevented alloy frames from catching on.

Wooden frames had been employed by a few makers during the 1890s, and an Italian maker toyed with the idea of re-introducing them during the 1950s, but nothing more has been heard of the idea, nor of the proposed use of plastics. But experiment continues, and the English rider Peter Duker, who in 1971 cycled around the world and crossed the American continent in record time, has recently been road-testing a machine made out of the light metal titanium by a British company.

When choosing a frame, remember to buy one which is not only attractive, well-made, light in weight yet rigid and meets your needs, but which is also of the correct dimensions. Long legs plus short body will necessitate a long seat-tube but a short top-tube; short legs plus long body will mean you will need a short seat-tube but a long top-tube. Too many people fall into the trap of only considering the question of saddle-height when choosing a frame.

Remember, too, that a frame slightly on the

Many materials have been employed in the manufacture of bicycles, including wood, as in this relic of a turn-of-the-century frame

small side (thus allowing about 5–6 inches of seat pin to show) will be more aesthetically pleasing to the eye than one which is slightly too big.

In choosing the correct size, bear the following points in mind:

It isn't enough simply to ascertain that you can touch the ground, tip-toe, with both feet. A track bike needs a high bottom bracket so that pedals do not hit the ground on steep bankings; this means that you might not be able to touch the ground with both feet, even though your riding position is correct.

To find the correct frame height, a good rule of thumb is to deduct ten inches from your inside-leg measurement.

On a bike built up ready for the road, you can find the correct position in the following manner: raise or lower the saddle until, seated in the saddle and with the pedal at its lowest point, you can place the heel of your foot on the pedal comfortably with your leg almost fully extended.

As for handlebar reach, this is very much a question of personal preference and once the correct saddle height has been found, it can be ascertained by finding where your hands most naturally fall for comfort. As a starting guide, get hold of a vertical mirror and a friend to hold you up so that you can see your position in it. Then incline forward till you are at about 45 degrees from the horizontal, with arms bent very slightly, as in normal riding position when they act as shock absorbers through this bending. Holding the bottom curves of the handlebars, you now have a correct position and can fit the appropriate choice of handlebar and stem accordingly.

For leisurely touring work, the bars can be raised slightly; for track racing they will need to be lower, thus bringing your weight further over the front wheel, while at the same time the saddle should be raised half-an-inch or so. As a general rule, the lower the gearing you are going to use, the lower you can afford to sit.

Wheels

At one time, wood rims (usually made of bamboo) were quite popular, especially for racing on bumpy roads or in the mountains. This was because they showed greater resilience, gave a more comfortable ride and resisted buckling better than steel rims. In addition, they did not overheat with prolonged braking, a failing of steel rims which often leads to tyre blow-outs.

The advent of the alloy rim, which boasted all these advantages and more besides, put wood out of business, and today alloy is the most commonly used material and infinitely preferable to steel. There are three main types of rim.

1. The old 'Westwood' flat rim, used with rod brakes (which make connection with the underside of the rim) and found only on heavy roadster bikes.

2. 'Endrick' rims, which are of 'U' section, the brake blocks coming into contact with the sides of the rim. Like the 'Westwood', these rims are used with conventional wired-on tyres. With 'Endricks', these are usually of the high-pressure variety.

3. 'Sprint' rims. Designed for use with tubular tyres (which are known as 'sew-ups' in the USA and 'singles' in Australia). Sprint rims have a shallow bed, the tyre being affixed with the use of rim cement to aid its own gripping properties. As with the 'Endrick', brake blocks make contact with the rim sides.

Companies like AVA, Fiamme, Mavic, Weinmann and Scheeren all have good reputations for both 'Endrick' and 'Sprint' rims in light alloy.

On track-racing machines, as well as on cheap mass-produced machines, wheel-hubs are secured in the forks by the use of simple nuts. Far more sophisticated in design, and employed on most top-quality lightweights as well as all road-racing mounts, are quick-release hubs which have a spring-loaded skewer

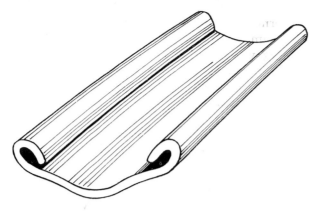

1 Westwood rim as employed on heavy roadster machines. The brakes operate on the under surface

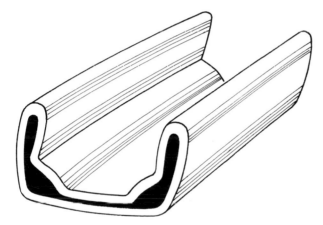

2 Endrick rim. Used in conjunction with high-pressure wired-on tyres. The braking surfaces are on the sides

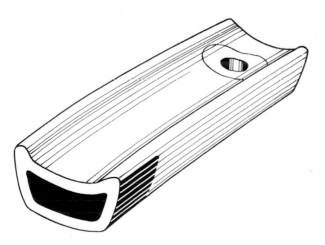

3 Sprint rim. Rubber glue is used to affix tubular tyres to the shallow bed of these rims. Tubulars must not be used with any other type of rim

running through a hollow axle. A simple flick of a cam-operated lever and the wheel drops clear of the fork-ends without the need of any fiddly tools, a boon for racing man and touring cyclist alike.

If price is no object, then Campagnolo hubs (of both the track and quick-release patterns) know no equal, but they are inordinately pricey and of recent years both Spanish (Zeus) and Japanese firms have produced remarkable copies which are hard to distinguish from the real thing both in appearance and quality, at a lower price. The French Simplex, Huret and Milremo hubs are also reliable but unfortunately the superb English hubs once marketed by Chater-Lea, Harden, Blumfield and B-H Air-lite are no longer manufactured.

As for spoking, double-butted chrome spokes are far and away the best, making for a strong wheel with an attractive appearance. (Robergel is the most reliable make.) The Continental practice of 36 spokes in each wheel is more sound than the English idea of 32 in the front wheel and 40 in the back. For specialist racing, such as track pursuiting and time-trialling over good roads, 24 or 28-spoked wheels may be employed but should be avoided for everyday use as they lack strength.

Tyres

The big debate in tyres is over the relative merits of wired-on (clincher) high-pressure tyres *versus* tubulars (sew-ups). Both types, in the now universally popular 27-inch size, are to be found on top-quality machines (though for racing, tubulars are always chosen).

Undoubtedly, the heavier wired-ons have better puncture-resistance, but they also mean added rolling-weight and it is this that makes cycling hard work—an ounce saved in the wheel department being worth pounds saved anywhere else on the machine.

When punctures do happen, the problem is worse with wired-ons, as they have to be repaired at the roadside, while the tubular-user can simply carry a complete spare tyre folded up small on the bike, and can effect a rapid tyre change, leaving the repair for more leisurely moments at home after completing the trip. Actually mending a punctured tubular is a job requiring a lot of patience and skill, and though puncture-repair services do exist these are costly. Moreover, punctures are more likely to spell irreparable damage to a tubular than a wired-on.

Should you decide on tubulars—and more and more people are doing so, even rough-stuff touring enthusiasts—buy the best you can afford. Heavier weight is no guarantee of increased puncture-resistance: the heavier tubulars are usually cheaper because they are of lower-quality construction. In my experience, a 9- to 10-ounce tubular of good quality (Barum

Kriterni, Pirelli Leggero, Clement or Vittoria, for example) is quite heavy enough, even for touring with quite a heavy load on roughish roads. I once toured Germany and the Swiss Alps in very wintry conditions without a spot of tyre trouble, despite riding seven-ounce tubulars of a type usually reserved for fast, short-distance racing on good roads.

A word of warning, though: if tubulars are your choice, then always carry at least one spare (or two if you are going to be away from home several days, as few ordinary cycle dealers carry stocks of such tyres) and make sure that your tyres are always securely cemented to the rim and cannot be rolled off.

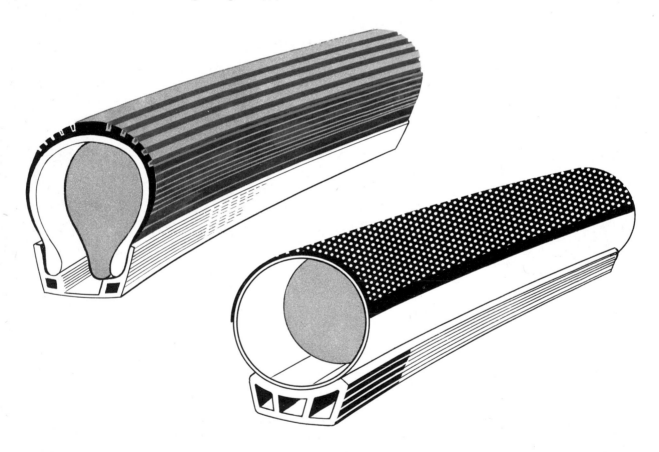

Wired-on tyres **left** have wire beading running through the edges to securely grip the rim. A rubber or cloth rim tape protects the inner-tube from abrasion by spoke ends

Tubular tyres **right** are used for racing. The inner tube is totally enclosed by the sewn-up outer casing. Such tyres may be changed in a matter of seconds, a spare being conveniently carried behind the saddle

Transmission
Pedals, Chain-set, Freewheel, Gears

Your bike's propulsion starts from the pedals and it is vital that you find a comfortable pair. Campagnolo are far and away the best quality (though, once again, Zeus make a near-perfect copy), but are rather narrow for use with anything but racing shoes.

For general riding, the wide choice of sturdy, low-priced pedals in the Lyotard range, made in France, should offer something for all requirements. Whatever your choice, it is as well to use all-metal rat-trap pedals, as the conventional rubber-tread pedal found on cheap machines provides a very insecure grip and can lead to a nasty accident should a foot slip off, something which is liable to happen frequently, particularly in wet conditions.

The pedals screw into the drive cranks, which are in turn affixed to the toothed front-sprockets of the transmission drive, called the chain rings. Cranks and chain rings together are known as the chain-set, and again Campagnolo lead the field with their finely-engineered cotterless sets in light alloy, although a rather disquieting number of crank breakages have been reported with this type.

Zeus, Williams and recently-introduced Japanese chain-sets, all patterned after the Campagnolo, are also fine—and far cheaper than the Italian produced 'brand-leader'—as are cotterless sets produced by the French TA and Stronglight concerns.

The once ubiquitous cottered sets are more trouble than they are worth and, since they are usually made of steel, tend to be inordinately heavy.

A good quality freewheel unit (Simplex, Regina, Moyne, Zeus and Milremo are all recommended) and chain (Sedis, Brampton, Reynolds, Regina being leading makes, while the chrome-finished Japanese chains are also reliable) will pay dividends in trouble-free service.

Cotterless, five-pin chainsets are a vast improvement on older and bulkier chainsets affixed with sloppy cotter-pins. This set is for an inch-pitch chain (note the wide gap between the teeth), which offers a stiffer transmission for track sprinting

27

Choice of gearing is very much a matter of the use to which your bike is going to be put. A derailleur is more suitable for the racing cyclist because of its lower rolling weight. Here again, Campagnolo is the finest quality you will get—at the highest price. Campagnolo's Record model gives exceptional chain-wrap and a smooth, positive change, while their cheaper Gran Sport and Sportsman gears are also extremely reliable in operation. The Japanese-made Sun Tour and the French-made Huret Allvit and Simplex Prestige models, all operating on the same parallelogram principle as the Campagnola, give a good change. For ultra-wide ratio gearing on touring bikes used in mountainous terrain, both Simplex and Huret market special models.

All these firms make front changers to pair up with their rear gear, enabling four, five or six speeds to be doubled or trebled by the use of two or three front chain-rings. Again, it is ·the more expensive models using the parallelogram

principle which give the best results.

Hub gears, such as the Sturmey Archer, have the advantage of being totally enclosed and are thus fully protected from the weather, needing little maintenance. However, they are not suitable for serious racing, since they offer only pre-ordained gear ratios, and, once they are a little worn, tend to slip.

As for hub gears, such as the Sturmey Archer, these have a certain following but offer only pre-ordained gear ratios. OK for utility riding or easy-paced touring, they are not much use for more serious work.

As for gear levers, most top European riders have now reverted to using down-tube control, arguing that the shorter cable-run gives more positive changing, but personally I prefer handlebar-end levers which enable changes to be effected in full flight, without removing one's hands from the bars. Provided that they are kept properly adjusted, these give a very neat change.

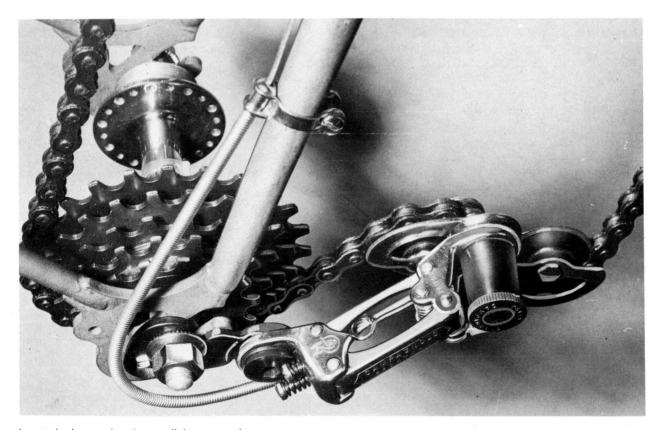

Increasingly popular, the parallelogram-action rear derailleur gear offers a positive change and smooth action

Brakes

As efficient transmission is vital for the easy propulsion of your bike, so good brakes with a smooth, reliable action are essential to ensure safe stops in emergency situations.

Undoubtedly, centre-pull cable-operated brakes give the smoothest stopping power and among them the well-proved Universal, Weinmann and Mafac Racer models command confidence. For heavily-loaded touring bikes, the brazed-on Mafac Criterium and Tandem models offer the ultimate in stopping power. However, there is now a side-pull calliper-action cable-brake which rivals the above mentioned centre-pulls in efficiency—manufactured, not surprisingly, by Campagnolo.

As for the levers, Campagnolo and Mafac best suit those with smaller hands while, if you have large hands, the Universal, Balilla and Weinmann models, fitted with rubber hoods, will offer you a more substantial grip.

Saddles or seats

Saddle, pedals and handlebars are the points of bodily contact with your machine and thus are of paramount importance when it comes to questions of comfort. To my mind, nothing can beat a carefully broken-in Brooks Professional leather saddle, which is beautifully shaped and has large-sized copper rivets to prevent the leather from tearing when it is softened up.

Breaking-in (softening the leather and shaping the saddle to suit your personal anatomy) is best achieved by rubbing saddle-soap, butter or Brooks' own special Proofide cream into the leather then carefully tapping the saddle lightly with a rubber hammer to 'work' the leather and render it supple, a process which takes many painstaking hours and requires great care, but is well worth all the trouble. The rest of the breaking-in process is achieved simply by usage.

Plastic saddles offer several advantages; they do not require breaking in, are impervious to the wet (a constant enemy of leather saddles) and are much lighter, but they offer less secure seating, tending to be slippery. This has been overcome by the recent introduction of leather and suede-covered saddles (of which the Unica is the best), while a quilted model offers increased comfort. Once an improved, leather-covered, plastic model can be offered with a shape which compares to the Brooks Professional, then even I will be won over from an all-leather saddle.

Whatever your choice, a Campagnolo, Nitor or similar seat-pillar with a built-in saddle-clip should be used, as saddle-slip is impossible with these.

A Weinmann side-pull calliper-action cable brake

Handlebars

Handlebars come in infinite variety and are a matter of personal taste, but the popular 'square-shaped' dropped handlebars such as the Maes, the Cinelli 'Giro d'Italia' and Cinelli 'Campione dell Mondo' models, plus the AVA range, all available in light alloy as well as steel, suit most people and combine well with an Ambrosio or Cinelli alloy stem.

Recent developments of more rigid alloys have removed the objections which most enthusiasts had at one time to alloy bars and stems, when the 'whip' produced on them was excessive, and they had an unfortunate tendency to deform after constant use.

Remember that the tops of dropped bars offer the same riding position as flat handlebars, while the dropped bend gives an alternative position which makes for less monotonous riding. If you do not want deeply-dropped racing bars, consider the shallower Randonneur.

Always use tape on your bars for improved grip and appearance. Remember, too, to plug the handlebar ends with rubber stops—this removes the danger of grazed knees. Dimpled plastic handlebar tape is cooler in use than cloth and stays cleaner, but many prefer the more positive grip afforded by the latter.

Lighting

The dynamo generator offers the finest lighting available (the Swiss-made Lucifer set is the most reliable I have ever used), and avoids the nuisance of batteries which always seem to go dead at the most inconvenient moment.

However, the generator does not produce light when the bike is stationary and this can lead to dangerous situations when you come to a halt at road junctions. There is also a drag inherent in the generator's power deriving from a roller which rubs against the tyre. In the wet, the roller is liable to slip, producing no light. Slip is avoided by the Surmey Archer Dynohub, which encases the generator inside the hub of the front wheel, but it still drags even when the lights are not in use, and also presents a 'rolling weight' problem.

Battery lights are less cumbersome and cause no drag, but they are unreliable in use and can be expensive to run if a lot of night-riding is to be done. A battery left on until all its power is exhausted will give eight or nine hours of light, whereas one used for some twenty minutes a night will run down more slowly as it re-charges when not in use. In such conditions, it is possible to get a total of over thirty hours light from a battery.

The simple truth is that there is no truly efficient lighting set available for cycles. You just have to make do with the poor choice available.

Mudguards or fenders

For some reason, most American cycling en-thusiasts eschew the use of mudguards, even for day-to-day riding and touring. It is an odd habit, because many an otherwise pleasant ride is ruined through a good soaking and the use of guards (fenders to Americans) involves little extra weight. Apart from racing and race-training, it is wise to use mudguards at all times, unless you are fortunate enough to reside in an area of extremely low rainfall.

The plastic guards tend to split easily, the stainless-steel Weinmann pattern, or the various deep-section French-made alloy guards, are the best bet. The short, so-called 'racing guards' fitted by many manufacturers to sports bikes are as good as useless, serving merely a rather dubious decorative purpose.

Bits and pieces

To complete your machine, you will need a sturdy, good-quality pump, preferably fitted with a push-on adaptor. High-pressure 'Presto' valves (as found on all tubulars and most high-pressure tyres) are to be preferred, though Schraeder valves offer the advantage that you can get them pumped up effortlessly at the local garage. However, special adaptors are available for use with Presto valves in that way.

A very useful item to carry is a Mafac tool-kit which is relatively light, contained in a con-venient plastic pouch, and enables you to carry

The old-fashioned Woods valve is hard to inflate and requires the use of a valve-rubber, which is liable to perish and lead to subsequent air-loss

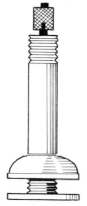

Universally employed on tubular tyres and usually found on European wired-ons, the Presta valve affords relatively easy in-flation and efficient air retention, but is liable to damage if the needle gets bent by clumsy usage. To pump the tyre, the small knob at the top must be loosened

Schraeder valves are simi-lar in principle to those found on automobiles and may be inflated from a filling station air-line

out most minor repairs at the roadside. If your choice is 'wired-ons', then don't forget to carry a puncture outfit and set of three tyre-levers.

Anyone in the habit of carrying packages should fit a sturdy panier support with removeable bags. Carriers are quite light, and a cape-roll (enclosing a puncture outfit and small toolkit) can be strapped on top. Many British riders use a small saddlebag, while others prefer the familiar 'musette' or shoulder-bag, adequate for carrying a cape, a little food and so on.

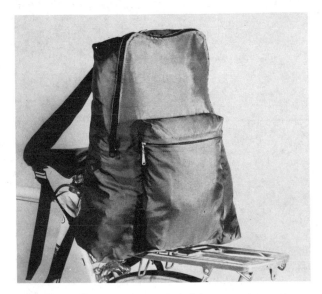

With the aid of weather-proofed bags such as these, substantial loads may be conveniently carried on a bicycle. It is advisable, for stability, to keep the weight low-slung and equally distributed. Supplementary front carriers are also available

Children's bicycles

As soon as a child is able to walk it is old enough to learn to cycle. Whether he or she should be allowed to cycle at such a tender age is another matter. When I was just eight, I rode the sixty-mile journey from my London home to the seaside resort of Southend and back along a main trunk road. Traffic conditions are very different today and any parent who allowed a small child to carry out such a hazardous cycle ride unaccompanied would be guilty of gross neglect of parental duty (not that my parents had given their blessing to my adventure—I had sneaked out unbeknown to them!).

Traffic hazards in modern cities and on main roads are now such that no child under the age of 12 is old or responsible enough to cope safely unless accompanied by an adult. But there are still plenty of places where a youngster can ride a bike and get a lot of fun out of it—quiet country lanes, special cycle-ways, parks where cycling is permitted, and the like.

Ownership of a first bicycle still remains the highpoint of many childhoods, and it is as well to make sure that the experience is a happy one by buying the correct machine for your child.

Never fall into the trap of getting an over-size bike because he or she 'will grow into it'. Quite apart from the greater danger of falling off, the effort of struggling with a bike that is too big will soon cause the child to tire of it and abandon the idea of cycling before ever discovering its joys. If for money reasons the bicycle has to last for several years, then there is still no cause to make this mistake, because there are now many machines available, especially small-wheelers, which offer an extremely wide range of adjustment.

For younger children, the simpler the bike is, the better. The complexities of multiple-gear shifting are too much for them to handle easily, and they will find it easier to cope with a back-pedalling 'coaster' hub-brake than with the lever-operated cable variety.

At the moment there is a great fad among children, both in the United States and Britain,

Children down through the years have delighted in their first bicycle. Today a wide choice is available and open-framed smallwheeler models such as these enable the machine to 'grow' with its rider thanks to the wide range of adjustment

Machines like this Raleigh Toledo with its sloping frame have been popular with generations of American children

Raleigh's Chopper model with its 'banana seat' saddle, high-rise handlebars and joystick gear lever has swept the childrens' market both in America and Britain, but would seem designed more as a forerunner to a first motorcycle than as an introduction to serious bicycling

Engineering ingenuity has made the bicycle a most versatile machine. This adaptation allows a child to take the back seat of his parent's tandem

for the chopper type of bicycle which several firms, notably Raleigh, have marketed with such enormous success. Loaded with gimmicky gadgets including the so-called 'banana-seat' elongated saddle, car-styled gear-shift, motorcycle-patterned crash-bars and so on, these bikes have certainly caught the youngsters' imaginations, but they are hardly likely to lead them into a more prolonged cycling career. What is more, the use of high-rise handlebars is both grotesque and dangerous. Since the rider has to reach up in the air for the grips, there is too little control over the steering, and youngsters using such handlebars are seen to wobble dangerously—hardly conducive to their introduction to good road sense.

A child can start cycling on a three-wheeler or with the aid of outrigger training wheels at the rear, but most will soon learn to keep their balance and will not need these aids for long.

Up to the age of eleven or twelve years, a solidly-constructed flat-handlebar bike is best (a 24- to 26-inch wheeled, 18- to 20-inch framed model suiting most nine to twelve-year olds) but after this age, many children are only too ready to graduate from treating a bicycle as a toy to more serious cycling activities.

Encouraging your child to want a scaled-down lightweight at this age, rather than a chopper type will help ensure that he retains an interest in the healthy pursuit of cycling for many years to come. As a teenager he is bound to want to go on longer, more adventurous rides and only a lightweight will enable him to do so

without undue fatigue, followed by frustration and loss of enthusiasm. Many companies now produce admirable lightweights in the smaller sizes. Indeed, scaled-down racing bikes are available for children as young as five years of age, though these are more a gimmick than anything else.

Remember that it is your duty to teach your child to ride competently with due consideration for the safety of others, as well as for his own life. It is equally important that he learns to maintain his bicycle in a roadworthy condition. Do not let him neglect his bike, allowing bright parts to rust and tyres to crack through under-inflation. Any child over the age of eight or nine is quite capable of pumping up his own tyres and mending his own punctures and should be encouraged to do so. Make sure your child's cycle is provided with adequate lighting if he is going to use it after dark. A few pennies spent on new batteries or bulbs may mean a life saved.

When buying your child's bike, ensure that he can comfortably reach the ground with both feet when seated in the saddle and that he does not have to overstretch in reaching forward for the handlebars. Check, too, that the brake-levers are within easy reach and can be applied without undue strain.

If your child is too old for stabiliser wheels but has never ridden a bike before, the best way to teach balance is to take him to a park or other quiet place off the main roads where there is a smooth and gentle downhill slope. First, get him to freewheel down the slope with

Something of an ultimate in touring machines with its wide-range 15-speed gearing, shallow-dropped handlebars, luggage carriers and dynamo lighting, this thoroughbred Jack Taylor model is seen here cleverly converted into a three-wheeled tandem

both feet scraping the ground, so that he can get the feel of his bike and its steering. When he has mastered directional stability, encourage him to repeat the manoeuvre with first one, then both feet on the pedals and, finally, while actually turning the pedals with his feet. A gentle hand on shoulder or saddle will help to inspire confidence in these initial stages. Once he has learned to ride in a straight line, set your child an obstacle course, involving low-speed turns and weaving between tin-cans or similar objects.

Most children will only require a couple of hours' tuition before they can cycle reasonably well. Some even ride straight off without any learning period, but bear it in mind that, as with most things, the older you are the more difficult it is to master the art—which is one very good reason for starting your children on cycling at an early age.

Finally, enrol your child in one of the cycling proficiency road-safety courses operated by most local authorities through the co-operation of the police and road safety organisations.

Tandems

Though the two-seater, or tandem, is nowhere near as popular as it once was, there is still a certain attraction in the machine and the sense of 'togetherness' it imparts to its riders, both of them sharing the work load and having no problems of keeping up with one another—though there may be complaints from one partner that the other is not doing his or her fair share of the pedalling!

Tandems are much faster than solo cycles on flat roads, but their awkwardness makes them slower up hills and harder to handle on twisting roads and in traffic.

In the early days, the 'sociable' or side-by-side machine enjoyed a spell of popularity, but today's tandems place one rider behind the other in an extension of a solo machine. With tandems, quality counts even more than usual, because of the heavy load to be carried, and a strong, rigid frame is essential. Not many firms make them these days but the British builder Jack Taylor specialises in them and his various models are available in the States through Wheel Goods Corporation. The best of his range is the sophisticated Touring model, which features 15-speed gearing, luggage carriers, alloy guards and faired-in lighting plus the extremely efficient Mafac Tandem brakes.

A few other companies still offer tandems, the French firm Gitane making one which has a man's style front section and an open-framed ladies' style for the rider at the rear. In tandem riding it is never a case of ladies first.

Look for good, strong wheels with heavy-gauge, double-butted spokes (36 in the front, 40 in the rear if possible) and substantial, wide-section tyres. With double the weight on board, firm brakes are also essential, the brazed-on Mafac Tandem brakes with their simple cantilever action being ideal.

Slower than the conventional bike, the tricycle never-theless demands some rather spectacular cornering techniques, particularly in competition use

Tricycles

To most people, the tricycle or three-wheeler, is a machine reserved for children and invalids but there is, in fact, a very enthusiastic following for 'the barrow', as it is popularly nicknamed in Britain.

Special races are organised and there is a strong Tricycle Association with a membership full of characters—you have to have some affinity for the bizarre to be attracted to tricycling, for such machines are slower than the bicycle and are apt to have somewhat unpredictable handling qualities, particularly on steep cambers and when descending hills.

To ride a trike requires the unlearning of everything that goes into riding a bike. You have to steer round corners rather than leaning round them and it is all too easy to bring one wheel off the ground and lose control. That said, they do provide a lot of fun and are far more tractable in winter conditions of snow and ice.

Tricycle manufacturers are few and far between these days, one or two American manufacturers turning out roadster models while in Britain, Jack Taylor produce lightweight models in small numbers and Holdsworth market a conversion kit which adapts an ordinary bike into a trike.

Some trikes are fitted with a differential in the rear axle, thus ensuring drive off both wheels, but cheaper models simply drive only one of the two rear wheels, the other spinning freely.

Tandem Tricycles

A rare hybrid of the two machines, the tandem trike is sometimes seen in British time trial racing. The awe-inspiring spectacle of a tandem-trike in full-flight round a bend in the wet is enough to give one nightmares for a long time afterwards.

Unicycles

Originally strictly a circus gadget, the one-wheeler or unicycle, has enjoyed a certain popularity in America of late with young and old alike. Although a unicycle is highly man-oeuvrable, it is strictly a plaything and not the thing for riding in traffic or for long-distance work!

Simplicity itself, the unicycle has become a popular 'toy' with children and adults alike.

Look Ma, no hands! Only one wheel, too, as this circus performer demonstrates the ultimate in skilful cycling. A world trick-cycling championship is held every year and bicycle-polo and cycle-ball are spectacular two-wheeled games

History

Cycling as a popular pursuit dates from the mid-nineteenth century but the germ of the idea was born long before that. In the quiet little English country church of Stoke Poges—also renowned as the inspiration for Gray's *Elegy*—there is a piece of stained-glass window, dating from the early sixteenth century, which depicts a cherub seated astride a wheeled bar which might be propelled by pushing forward with the feet. It seems to show that the artist was familiar with a type of 'hobby horse' resembling the 'célérifère', the invention of which is otherwise credited to one Comte de Sivrac, a French nobleman who introduced his machine to an astonished public at the Palais Royal Gardens, Paris, in 1791.

De Sivrac's 'invention'—in fact he almost certainly simply scaled-up what had for years been a recognised children's nursery toy—consisted of two wheels, in line, fashioned in the style of a wooden horse, complete with carved head. It could not be steered, except in minor deviations from the straight line effected by leaning it over to one side or the other.

Renamed the 'velocipede', this type of machine became quite fashionable in Parisian society, but its future was obviously limited until, in 1816, the German Baron Karl von Drais improved on the earlier machines by fitting a steerable front wheel, arm-rests to aid the transmission of pushing power, a padded seat for greater comfort and even a primitive rear-wheel brake.

So a new alternative to walking had been found. It was certainly faster, so long as the route to be covered was flat and reasonably well surfaced, but it was still very much a plaything, even though some ultra-enthusiastic pioneers were already tackling runs of up to fifty miles and averaging speeds of eight or nine miles an hour—a formidable achievement with such uncomfortable and inflexible mounts.

The stage was now set for the introduction of mechanisation to the propulsion of the device and, in 1821, an Englishman named Lewis Compertz hit on the idea of a rack-and-pinion device which added power produced by pushing and pulling with the arms to that already gained from pushing the feet along the ground.

Top A Célérifère of 1818, first introduced in 1791
Centre A Draisienne or 'Pedestrian's Accelerator', 1819
Bottom A Hobby-horse of 1818

The real breakthrough came though in 1839 when a twenty-nine-year-old Scottish blacksmith studied a 'hobby-horse' belonging to a friend and decided that he would himself construct two of them, one for his own use, the other for a workmate.

Soon tiring of the cumbersome method of propulsion then extant, Macmillan, who was quickly nicknamed Daft Pate by his sceptical neighbours, fitted a pair of hanging stirrup-pedals attached to long cranks which drove the rear wheel. It was an early form of shaft-drive, more akin to that used in steam railway locomotives than to the modern chain-driven bicycle, but it was a beginning.

By increasing the size of the rear (drive) wheel, the Scotsman effectively raised the gearing of the machine, which in turn led to yet higher speeds. Indeed, Macmillan made further cycling history when at the end of a forty-mile spin to Glasgow in 1842 he ran down a small child and became the first cyclist to be hauled in front of the courts, being fined five shillings by the Gorbals' magistrates for his reckless riding.

Macmillan's machine, which weighed in at a monstrous 67 pounds, was primitive in both concept and construction, but it pointed the way by now enabling a cyclist to ride without having to put his feet to ground to propel him on his way.

It was to be a further twenty years before the bicycle boom really got under way, and it was thanks to Pierre Michaux's far more effective, and simpler, idea of propelling a machine merely by affixing cranks to the axle of the front wheel. Pierre Lallement, one of Michaux's employees, claimed that it was actually he who had come up with the idea, and not his boss. In 1863, he left Michaux's company and travelled to the USA, where he filed the first American bicycle patent and also concluded a manufacturing deal with a firm in Connecticut.

The Paris Exhibition of 1867 saw the 'boneshaker', as it was still called by the cynics, already an established mode of transport. Indeed, Michaux, who started production in 1861 with just two sales, had recently opened a new factory employing three hundred workmen, so staggering had been the success of his innovations.

Soon three-wheeled, four-wheeled, tandem

Top Kirkpatrick Macmillan and his Dandy-horse, the first rear-driven bicycle. **Centre** The Michaux Velocipede. **Bottom** A racing 'boneshaker' of 1869

39

(both in-line and two-abreast) and even triplet versions of the velocipede hit the market. They were propelled in a variety of fashions, using leg-power, arm-power and even, in one instance, power generated by two dogs caged inside the enormous drive-wheels and working treadmill fashion to ensure forward motion!

Schools sprang up in major cities both in Europe and America where the gentry could learn the art of cycle riding and stunts like 'no hands', standing on the saddle and so on. The Michaux Cycle Club, for instance, was housed in an elegant brownstone building in New York, where waiters served drinks to fashionable ladies and gentlemen as they watched the riders circling the riding rink.

Racing became the fashion, too, the first recognised and organised race being held in the Parc St. Cloud, Paris on 31 May, 1868. Run over a two-kilometre course in front of an enormous crowd on a blazing hot day, the race was won by Dr. James Moore. Born at Bury St. Edmunds in 1849, he had spent most of his life in France where his father, a veterinary surgeon, had settled. For his efforts, Moore received a handsome gold medal bearing the image of Emperor Napoleon III.

A year later, the first true road-race was held:

Paris-Rouen (held to this day as an annual amateur classic) and Moore was again victorious. Some 323 riders had entered and 200 actually started from the French capital where the current Miss America gave the starting signal.

Before starting, Moore had told his friends: 'I shall either win or kill myself trying, in which case you will find my body on the road.' But at the finish the Englishman had three-quarters of an hour lead over runner-up Castera, who was, in turn, thirty minutes ahead of the next man.

Moore went on to win five world championships and took the English one-mile title on the Molyneux ground, better known today as the home of the Wolverhampton Wanderers' soccer club.

Soon cycle-racing tracks were springing up all over the place as the new sport attracted growing numbers of adherents.

By the 1870s, the desire for greater speeds led to the development of the high bicycle, today known to collectors as the Old Ordinary and to the general public by the slightly derogatory term 'penny farthing', because its large front-wheel and small rear-wheel resembled the relationship between those two coins of the British realm.

The bigger the drive wheel, the bigger the

VELOCIPEDES.

WOOD BROTHERS,

596 Broadway, New York,

Manufacturers of fine Pleasure Carriages, are now prepared to receive orders for the celebrated

PARISIAN VELOCIPEDES,

of their own manufacture, which for durability and beauty of finish are not equaled.

gear and thus the greater the speed potential of the bicycle concerned. Some real monsters soon appeared on the market. Riding these machines could be extremely hazardous. They took much agility to mount, since the huge wheel had to be held steady, and a bump in the road could send the unfortunate rider sprawling from a height of five or more feet, often at considerable speed. Descending hills was a thrilling experience. Footrests were fitted high on the front forks so that the rider could free his feet from the fast-spinning pedals and give the machine its head.

Rowley Turner, the Paris agent of the Coventry Sewing Machine Co., brought his native city to cycling prominence. In 1869, he invited half-a-dozen people to attend a demonstration in Old Street, St. Luke's. One of them wrote later:

A foreign-looking packing case was brought in. As it was opened I recognised a piece of apparatus consisting mainly of two wheels, similar to one I had seen not long before in Paris, but the one I saw in Paris was much smaller; the lad being mounted on it, who drove the machine by placing his feet on the ground. I looked upon it as a mere jouet-d'enfant such as the Parisians are so clever in designing. It produced but little impression on me and certainly did not strike me as being a new means of locomotion. A slender young man

who I soon came to know as Mr. Turner of Paris followed the packing-case and superintended its opening; the gymnasium was cleared, Mr Turner took off his coat, grasped the handles of the machine and with a short run, to my intense surprise, vaulted on to it and, putting his feet on the treadles, made a circuit of the room. We were some half-a-dozen spectators and I shall never forget our astonishment at the sight of Mr. Turner whirling himself round the room, sitting on a bar above a pair of wheels in a line that ought, as we innocently supposed, to fall down immediately he jumped off the ground. Judge then of our greater surprise when instead of stopping by tilting over on one foot, he slowly halted and, turning the front-wheel diagonally, remained quite still, balancing on the wheels.

With the sewing machine trade in recession and French velocipede makers unable to meet the demand for their machines, Turner was readily able to persuade his firm to turn to cycle manufacture and immediately secured an order to export four hundred machines to France, the very country which had previously supplied his own needs. However, the outbreak of the Franco-Prussian War in 1870 caused a cancellation of the order and Turner had to market the machines on the home market instead, a move which

41

gave birth to a thriving British cycle industry, which still led the world a century later, though its centre had moved by then from Coventry to Nottingham. The development of this new industry saved many Midland firms from impending disaster, as they were able to switch their efforts from depressed trades to this burgeoning new line.

One of the leading lights of the Coventry cycle trade and a prodigious inventor was James Starley who, for his Ariel high bicycle, perfected the first all-metal cycle wheel. In the urgent quest for increasingly high speeds, the front drive-wheel got bigger and bigger (some even reaching sixty inches in diameter), to the absolute limit of the rider's inside leg measurement.

Popular though it was, however, the high bicycle was doomed. Yet bigger gears were obviously called for and could only be achieved by revolutionary methods. In 1885 Starley invented the 'safety' bicycle which sported wheels of just thirty inches diameter, the rear-wheel being driven by a chain so that the gearing could be raised or lowered by the simple expedient of switching the sizes of the front chain-wheel and the rear sprocket. It was, to all effects, the basis of the bicycle as we know it today, any further refinements to come being of detail rather than in the overall concept.

Actually, Starley's invention seems to have been pre-dated by that of a French clockmaker named André Guilmet, who had hit on the same idea more than a decade earlier but was killed in the Franco-Prussian War before he had a chance to demonstrate his bicycle's worth. In fact, it was not even known about until somebody opened up a loft many years later and found it lying there, forgotten.

H J Lawson, another native of Coventry, had also beaten Starley to it, making a chain-driven cycle in 1873, but he seems to have been singularly lacking in business sense, for after taking a further eleven years to perfect his machine and bring it to the attention of the BSA company, in an attempt to persuade them to put it into production, they politely declined and then promptly marketed a machine of their own, patterned to a remarkably similar design.

'Mr Henry Davies, USA bicyclist' reads the terse inscription on this study of an early enthusiast and his mount

R. J. McCreedy astride one of the first Old Ordinary bicycles to be fitted with pneumatic tyres after their invention by John Boyd Dunlop of Belfast

Right from the early days, women joined in wheeled activities, though etiquette required a modest and rather inconvenient mode of dress, in contrast to the man's tight breeches and knee stockings seen in this picture from 1874

In America, a thriving cycle industry had become established, thanks largely to Colonel A A Pope of Boston, Massachusetts, a carriage-maker and retired Union Army Officer who first imported British high-wheelers in 1876. Two years later he went into production himself.

Hired to demonstrate the machine in New York, 28-year-old Will Pitman, former Maryland boneshaker champion, got himself arrested for frightening a horse. The resultant publicity was a godsend for Pope's Columbia machine, especially when the 'Sun' newspaper's editor, Willian Dana, sprang to Pitman's defence.

Pope's company soon became the largest in the world—a position later usurped by the British Raleigh colossus—and introduced the principles of mass-production which would later be used to such world-shaking effect by the automobile industry. Sponsoring races, campaigning for better roads, and a prime mover in the foundation of the League of American Wheelmen, Pope was as important a figure to the American industry as Starley was in Britain.

By the 1880s, cycling was a fashionable pursuit.

THE ROVER SAFETY BICYCLE (PATENTED).

Safer than any Tricycle, faster and easier than any Bicycle ever made. Fitted with handles to turn for convenience in storing or shipping. Far and away the best hill-climber in the market.

Rather a bizarre-looking machine, this 1885 Rover Safety was nevertheless the forerunner of the chain-driven bicycle we know today

In England, the Bishop of Chelmsford held the Essex sprint crown, the nobility and gentry rode for leisure and raced on the country's many tracks and the Prince of Wales was a regular spectator at the races.

Despite opposition from horse-and-carriage drivers who were not averse to giving a good whipping to any cyclist who had the temerity to overtake them, the bicycle was the new king of the road and a further leap forward was taken when an Irish veterinary surgeon named Dr. John Boyd Dunlop invented the first pneumatic tyre as an aid to comfort on his son's tricycle, using rubber sheeting and strips of linen from one of his wife's old dresses as raw materials. William Hume of the Belfast Cruisers' Cycling Club persuaded Dunlop to make him a similar pair of tyres for his racing machine and then set out and crushed the local opposition in a race on 18 May 1889.

Sensing the commercial value of his invention, Dunlop went into the tyre manufacturing industry and within a few years the pneumatic had supplanted the solid tyre as standard

John Boyd Dunlop, the father of the modern rubber industry, revolutionised bicycling when he invented the pneumatic tyre, though he had no such thing in mind: he simply wanted to make his son's pedalling more comfortable!

equipment and the Dunlop company had become the largest in the tyre business.

A further stride was taken when the freewheel appeared in 1896, enabling cyclists to coast downhill with their feet on the pedals. Multiple gearing appeared shortly afterwards, both primitive derailleur 'chain-shift' mechanisms employing several sprockets of varied size, and the Sturmey-Archer hub gear.

Cycle sales flourished, the craze reaching such proportions that other trades complained of suffering severe recession; people were said to be too busy cycling to want to read books, play pianos or engage in other previously popular pursuits.

Thousands of firms were engaged in cycle manufacture, more than five hundred in America alone, and countless inventors busied themselves with perfecting the machine which had brought new liberty of movement to the populace. The cycle manufacturing trade was a breeding ground of great engineering and industrial advances in aviation and motoring. It was from a background of cycle shops at the turn of the century that Wilbur and Orville Wright and Glenn Curtiss created their flying machines, and Henry Ford and William Morris (later Lord Nuffield) their automobile empires. The trade marks Humber, Singer, Peugeot, De Dion and Rover all made their original appearance on the frames of bicycles.

Cycling was by no means merely a male pursuit. One lady, by name Mrs Bloomer, added a new word to the English language and stirred up amazing reactions—the like of Women's Lib today—when she and her friends appeared in the revolutionary divided skirts (or 'bloomers') she designed to make cycling a safer and easier practice than it was when trying to keep the long skirts of the day out of spokes and chains.

Cycling still found opponents in those early days. Some hostelries refused to serve cyclists who came in dishevelled and dirty after a spin on the dusty, bumpy, loose-surfaced and mud-strewn roads of the pre-motoring era. Country bumpkins took great delight in thrusting sticks into passing wheels or spreading nails, tacks or broken glass over the road, while farmers would block roads with their carts.

Opel was just one of many famous motor manufacturers who started off in the cycle industry. Ford, Morris, Peugeot, Sunbeam, Triumph and Humber were others

The caption of a cartoon which appeared in an early edition of the magazine 'Cycling' (founded in 1891 and still published in London today) reveals the attitude of many policemen and justices:

Magistrate Splitz-Splutter: *Another cyclist Snooks? How did you catch the reptile?'*

Constable X 1002: '*Well, yer Wushup, we see'd him coming up without his lamp and tried to rake him off with a stick but he shot by an' just got clear of Watkins' lasso. I broke his head with me truncheon but even then we'd have lost him if he hadn't ran foul of the rope we keeps across the road.'*

In 1878, an English enthusiast of the wheeled sport named Stanely Cotterell was prompted to call into being the Bicycle Touring Club. In 1883, it became the Cyclists Touring Club, an organisation every bit as active in the 1970s as it was in that pioneering era a hundred years ago.

Not only does the CTC provide a sociable local organisation with District Associations which organise club runs, tours, social functions and so on, but it provides an information and advice service and keeps a watching brief on the protection of cyclists' interests through lobbying both in Parliamentary and local government circles.

The most important victory in the organisation's history occurred when it fought for the passing of the Local Government Act, popularly known as the Cyclists' Magna Carta, which removed the previous powers granted to local authorities under the 1878 Highway and Railway (Amendment) Act under which they had been able to impose highly restrictive conditions on cyclists, in some instances even forbidding them from using public highways altogether.

Another major victory came when the CTC brought a successful action against the proprietor of the Hautboy Hotel in Surrey, who had refused service in the coffee room, to Lady Harbeton, one of the club's prominent members, offering to serve her in the bar parlour instead, an unforgivable slight to a lady of breeding in those days. The proprietor was indicted for 'Wilfully and unlawfully neglecting and refusing to supply a traveller with victuals'.

After visiting the CTC's Liverpool headquarters in 1888, a highly-impressed party of

The introduction of 'bloomers' made cycling easier for the ladies, but the glimpse of stockinged knees shocked the prudes and caused not a little scandal at the time

American enthusiasts returned home and formed the League of American Wheelmen, whose membership reached an impressive 100,000 during the 1890s, but plummeted to a mere 8000 by 1902, a victim, as indeed was the bicycle itself, of the advent of the horseless carriage.

Like the CTC, the new American body fought for cyclists' rights. Its two most renowned triumphs were in the Haddonfield Turnpike Case, a test case which secured the rights of cyclists to use inter-state highways, and the eight-year battle against the ban on cyclists in New York's Central Park.

Cyclists were carrying out many remarkable feats of endurance by the end of the century. In 1884, Thomas Stevens, mounted on a cumbersome high bicycle, took 103½ days to become the first cyclist to cross the United States from the Pacific to the Atlantic coast, and ten years later a young American girl named Annie Londonberry rode around the world. This feat was emulated by William Workman and his wife Fannie, daughter of a Massachusetts' State Governor, who spent a decade touring around the world by a highly indirect route, which led to a series of fascinating books describing their adventures, and still worth reading today.

On the European Continent, today's great classic cycle races, Paris-Roubaix, Paris-Tours, Milan-San Remo, Tour of Lombardy and others were already established as major sporting events, while English riders were fascinated by the challenge of the End-to-End, the Lands End to John O'Groats record route which ran from the south-west tip of England to the north-east of Scotland. Road-racing was prevented from developing as it did on the Continent by police opposition to massed starts. This led instead to the invention of the time trial, still the major form of road competition in Britain.

Since the police were in the habit of pouncing on any group of speeding cyclists and charging them with 'riding furiously so as to endanger the life and limb of passengers upon the Queen's highway.' The pioneer racing man and official, F T Bidlake, hit on the idea of dispatching riders individually at one-minute intervals, each rider being required to cover the prescribed route alone and without pace, the winner being the rider who covered the distance in the shortest time.

To avoid arousing police suspicions of racing, riders were required to 'dress inconspicuously', carried no numbers (they shouted them out to officials *en route* and at the finish) and were sworn to secrecy, publicity being strictly avoided. Start sheets bore the legend 'strictly private and confidential'. Courses were refered to by code numbers known only to cyclists and every effort was made to keep the sport as undercover as possible. Its subsequent popularity seems all the more amazing!

A group of British enthusiasts, who had enjoyed trips to continental races during the 1930s, hankered after proper road-racing. Massed-starts on the open road being banned by the official controlling bodies of the sport in Britain, and their enthusiasm for bunched racing was only partially satisfied by massed-start races held on airfields and motor-racing circuits such as Brooklands and Donnington Park. These enthusiasts, led by the redoubtable Percy Stallard, took the opportunity offered by the relatively traffic-free roads of war-time to put on the first true road-race for nearly half a century on 7 June 1942.

The historic race ran from Wolverhampton to Llangollen and back and brought down immediate suspensions upon the heads of the officials and the participants. Their answer was to form the dissident British League of Racing Cyclists in 1942, and to promote their own programme of races.

They were accused of jeopardising the whole future of the sport, of taking an unfair advantage of other cyclists who were serving in the forces overseas and who would, it was suggested, return home after the war to find that all cycle racing on public roads had been banned.

But the BLRC persisted, drawing its riders from among servicemen on leave, refugees from the continent, and men excused military service or stationed at home. Taking a continental approach, they carried racing to the public, attracted sponsorship from commercial firms and introduced cash racing, while Road Time Trials Council events stayed 'amateur only'.

Percy Stallard defied the staid British cycling authorities to reintroduce bunched road-racing to Britain in 1942. He practised the sport as well as organising it; here he wins the 1944 Circuit of the Wrekin

It was a long, hard fight and great bitterness, sometimes even open violence, was generated by the quarrelling within the sport, but the BLRC proved its point when, in the 1956 Road Traffic Act, Parliament allowed cycle racing on the public highway, under controlled conditions. The final battle won, the BLRC amalgamated with the old National Cyclists Union to form the British Cycling Federation which, today controls road racing and track sport in Great Britain. Time-trialling remains the province of the still essentially more conservative Road Time Trials Council.

There is no doubt that, but for the courageous pioneering of Percy Stallard and his associates, British cycling would still be a back-water instead of a prospering sport which produces riders who can challenge the Continentals.

Fears that road-racing with its riders starting in a bunch would end with the sport being entirely banned from the roads have proved groundless. In fact, during the entire existence of the BLRC there was only one fatal accident in a road race, while in time-trialling, held by its nature on fast and busy main roads, this figure was, unhappily, greatly exceeded.

Although time trials are run in other countries, it is only in Britain that they are regarded almost as a sport apart, competition being over prescribed distances or times—10 miles, 25 miles, 30 miles, 50 miles or 100 miles; 12 hours or 24 hours—with a beating of a personal best time counting for more, in most riders' eyes, than their placing in the event.

It was only gradually that time-trialling emerged from the shadows. With thousands of riders taking part each weekend, its existence was hardly a secret, despite the mystification. The originally-specified 'inconspicuous dress' of black tights and black tight-fitting, long-sleeved 'Alpaca jacket', which may have attracted little notice around 1900, could hardly have been more conspicuous by the 1930s, but traditions die hard and it was not until well after World War 2 that coloured club jerseys, shorts, race numbers, advance publicity and other innovations were accepted.

Despite all the repressions which cycling sport suffered in its early days, by the beginning of the twentieth century, the bicycle had already assumed the wide variety of roles it fills today: as a simple, efficient and inexpensive mode of transportation, as a sporting machine, as a pleasant way of touring the countryside and as a means of ensuring good health through a far from unpleasant exercise.

There were still a few doubting Thomases, and some doctors, perhaps influenced by the hernias, bruises and headaches which had been commonplace among riders of the cumbersome old boneshakers and high bicycles on the atrocious roads, still believed cycling to be a risk to health, and warned, absurdly, of the dangers of heart-strain and over-exertion. Today, the only real health dangers inherent in cycling are those arising from inhaling polluted air in our traffic-clogged cities, and the safety risks derive from that same traffic. The bicycle is, however, a highly manoeuvrable machine and the competent rider is well equipped to avoid accidents, it being far simpler to get out of the way on a bike than it is in a car which can often rely on nothing more than a good set of brakes, when the bike can take to the sidewalk or dive through the narrowest of gaps. As for inhaling polluted air, well the cyclist can often strike off down less-used side-streets where there is a better chance of escaping the fumes of busy traffic.

49

A piece of stained-glass window in Stoke Poges church, Buckinghamshire, England shows that, as far back as the 16th Century, the idea of a two-wheeled, foot-propelled vehicle was being formulated

Whether for nostalgia or as pure fun, there is a considerable market today for replicas of the old high bicycle, which are being turned out in thousands by a couple of British manufacturers

Bicycling had its perils in the days of the old Ordinary, as is pointedly illustrated by this period music sheet **opposite**

It was President Eisenhower's physician, Dr Paul Dudley White, who first focussed publicity on the health-giving aspects of cycling, and over the past decade or so it has been this aspect which has attracted millions of people back to the machine which they had abandoned once they were old enough to drive a car. They suddenly rediscovered forgotten pleasures, enjoyed new convenience, saved money and played a part in helping to reduce the ecological dangers of which the world has at last become aware.

We may be in for a repetition of what happened at the turn of the century. By then, cycling had ceased to be the amusement of Society, the new-fangled automobile having won their fickle attentions, and had assumed a more utilitarian and humble role. Not only did millions rely on the bicycle to carry them to work, but many used it in their work as well. Policemen, postmen, delivery boys and many others relied on the bicycle to help them carry out their daily tasks, and the military, too, took a keen interest in the bicycle's potential.

As early as 1870, the Italian army equipped each of its regiments with four bicycles apiece, while by the 1890s, the French had developed a folding bike which could be carried on a soldier's back. Hindsight teaches us that its role was to be a limited one, as foreseen by H G Wells who, like his literary sparring-partner George Bernard Shaw, was an enthusiastic cyclist. In spite of the development by the US army of a tricycle armed with a handlebar-mounted machine gun, and the invention of other ingenious war machines, Wells predicted that the bicycle could not possibly play a decisive role in future wars as an auxiliary to cavalry or infantry, but should be utilised, quite simply, as a light form of transport, especially in difficult terrain where it could easily be manhandled when actual riding was impossible.

As late as World War 2, the bicycle was used in just such a fashion, paratroopers being equipped with folding bikes to increase their mobility on landing, while cycle-mounted orderlies played a valuable role. The bicycle has also found a use in modern guerilla warfare, many of the lightning raids by the IRA in Ireland and the Viet Cong in Vietnam having been executed on

Centre British infantry riding back to the trenches on bicycles in 1917. **Bottom** The quest for the perfect bicycle continues. This 73-year-old retired British motor fitter built his horizontal bike to reduce wind resistance, but found it an unstable mount

this unobtrusive and nearly silent vehicle.

Just as the function of the bicycle had already become clear with the advent of the twentieth century, so has its basic design. A number of revolutionary departures have been tried since then—such as the recumbent bicycle (on which the rider lay flat on his stomach for streamlining), the shaft-driven bike, and the closed-in bike with an all-enveloping fairing—yet the diamond-framed, chain-driven bicycle familiar to our grandparents is still used today with only improvements of detail.

Many variations of frame design have been tried, among the more notable innovations being the Dursley Pederson, which was constructed somewhat on the principle of the suspension bridge with small-gauge tubes held under tension by an array of steel wires; the Hetchins, with its curly rear-stays, for which the makers claimed benefits in freedom from 'whip' the Bates, with its oddly-shaped front forks and the Paris with its open frame lay-out. In spite of them all, the familiar diamond frame design has won through as being the most practicable.

The new gadgets of which cycling magazines have always been full are usually detail improvements on earlier inventions: lighter, stronger materials, design refinements on previously crude accessories—all these factors have helped to refine the machines of the 1970s.

For instance, the derailleur chain-shift multi-gearing system has only come into general usage and reached mechanical near-perfection since World War 2, but it was, as we have seen, actually invented almost immediately after the freewheel first came into use.

Steeper frame angles, shorter wheelbases and lighter wheels and tyres have all become possible with the making of smoother roads. This has led to more effortless cycling, making the twenty-pound lightweight of today a thorough-bred in comparison with the fifty to sixty-pound monster of 1900. But it remains a fact that improved braking, better transmission, smoother steering, more responsive handling, greater comfort and higher speed potential have all been achieved simply by perfecting component parts which were already familiar seventy years ago.

S F Edge, **middle**, with a Rudge Whitworth cycle in later years, was an early pioneer road-record breaker who went on to win some of the earliest motor races Alex Moulton, **above**, has won renown for the small-wheel bicycle which bears his name and, thanks to its convenience, brought thousands back onto wheels

The one radical change in the concept of cycling has not been in the machine itself but in the use to which it is put. No longer are the streets full of people plodding wearily to and from work on old, rusty, neglected machines simply because they cannot afford other forms of transport. Today's cyclist rides a bike through choice rather than through necessity. He has an eye on the health-giving aspects, and maybe regards using a bike as his small contribution in the fight against the pollution which motor transport has brought into our lives, and enjoys the inexpensive freedom of movement which cycling gives him. Pleasure is most decidedly the emphasis in cycling today, whether it is derived from a simple ten-mile jaunt in the country, an ambitious 1000-mile holiday tour or a tough but exhilarating 100-mile race.

Beginnings

Riding a bike is pretty basic; riding it *properly* is something else. Frankly, it is amazing how many people who have been cycling all their lives have no idea just how much easier and more pleasant they could make their riding. For a start, of course, you need the right machine; secondly, you need to ride it the correct and most economical way; and thirdly you need to dress right for it.

How then does one ride properly? Half the battle, once you've learned the basics of steering and balance, is in mastering the art of efficient pedalling. Never, but *never*, ride with the arch of your foot on the pedal. Always use the ball of your foot, for that way you make best use of your leg muscles which are, after all, the engine of your bicycle.

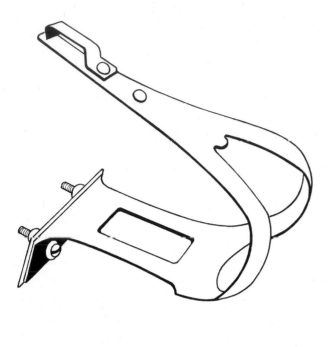

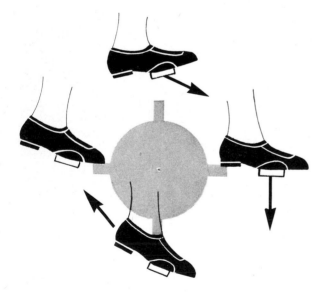

The use of toe-clips together with straps and shoeplates (which have slots to engage the rear edge of the pedal) facilitate the 'ankling' method of pedalling in which the foot claws its way past the top and bottom dead-centre positions, and also lifts the pedal on its upward stroke, thus ensuring the transmission of power through the entire 180°

One beauty of using toeclips and straps is that you have no option in the matter, your feet are bound to place themselves properly—provided that you have the right length clips. Toeclips are made in three sizes—small, medium and large. The small size is only really of use to ladies with very small feet, while you should not use large clips unless you take size nine shoes or upwards. Unfortunately, too many cyclists start off with long clips and get into the habit of using them, finding it very difficult to change over to medium size later on.

The truth is that, for most people, medium clips will ensure the smoothest pedal action. The art is to 'stroke' the pedal round rather than just pushing up and down. 'Ankling', as it is known, ensures that effort is being transmitted to the pedals not only on the way down but also at top and bottom dead-centre. With the aid of clips, the pedals can actually be pulled up, as well as thrust down (see illustration).

For pedalling to be efficient, gearing must be right. Today there is a tendency in Britain to use higher and higher gears, 'windmills' as they are known, with gearing of 118 inches not being unknown in time-trialling circles. On the other hand, most American riders tend to undergear to an exaggerated extent, seeming to feel it a crime ever to climb out of the saddle to tackle a rise. Yet occasional out-of-the-saddle work, 'dancing' on the pedals, helps to alleviate tedium and gives muscles a chance to stretch out in a different fashion which is a way of avoiding cramp.

Find a gear which gives a certain resistance yet never feels sluggish. Big gear or small, the idea is to pedal with what the French call 'souplesse', or suppleness, rather than forcing the pedals round in a laboured fashion or pedalling so rapidly as to bounce in the saddle, thus losing power.

Always change down slightly before hitting a rise. Gear changing while actually climbing uphill tends to lead to rough changes with much crunching and grinding and the danger of a broken chain. You must never stop pedalling while in the process of changing gear (except with a hub-type). Always conserve momentum —not wasting energy already expended.

Children should be encouraged to maintain their own
machines, thus engendering the complete independence
which the pursuit of cycling offers them

Bright sunshine, a picturesque leafy lane—the delights
of the countryside are opened to the child who has his
own bicycle and the mobility it brings

Proper tuition in the mechanical aspects of bicycling as
well as in road safety will ensure that the great
adventure will be enjoyed to the fullest

When going downhill, do not brake over-much. The steering of a machine under braking is not as accurate as that of one under power. Try to anticipate situations; do not just watch the vehicle in front, keep an eye on those up the road, too.

On a switchback road, speed held downhill helps you get halfway up the other side, so why waste it by freewheeling when it is possible to maintain your speed by a little easy pedalling?

When going into a corner, think ahead; do not brake in the corner but when approaching it, then let the brakes off as you go round it, as this makes skids and loss of control less likely.

Though you do not have to treat every ride as a race, journeys to and from work will be less tedious if tackled at a brisk romp. Plodding along can be very demoralising. Of course, you don't need to work up a sweat, but keep rolling.

Choose your routes with care. Look for roads you have not travelled before, try detours down side roads rather than sticking to main thoroughfares where traffic makes cycling not only unpleasant and dirty but downright dangerous.

For general utility riding, a bike with a low bottom-bracket will make for easier halts in traffic, as you can place your feet on the ground comfortably when stopping, while keeping the right saddle height for optimum pedalling efficiency.

A large bell or a horn will help ensure safety though many riders find it more effective to rely on a bellowing pair of lungs.

Dogs are a problem in many countries. An accurately-wielded pump is a great deterrent to their attentions, while in the USA it is possible to buy a dog-repellent spray.

This boy's saddle is a little too low and he is rather stretched out in reaching the handlebars. He is demonstrating a rather sloppy style and pedalling with the arch instead of the ball of the foot

If the right size of machine is used and the technique can be mastered, a child is never too young to start bicycling. However, never let your child ride on the highway without proper tuition and supervision

These students find their bikes are ideal low-cost transport, with baskets that are handy for books or shopping

A simple obstacle course tests a child's bike control and reactions. Bicycling proficiency tests are now organised by many local authorities with the full co-operation of schools and police forces

Schoolboy racing is now a recognised school activity in Britain and in other countries, too, youngsters of as little as eight years of age can compete in properly-supervised competitions.

Before the start, machines are examined for road-worthiness

Despite the vagaries of climate, properly-equipped
bicycle tourists can enjoy themselves, especially when
in the company of like-minded enthusiasts

Always allow plenty of time for your trips, leaving something in hand for inclement weather, punctures and mechanical trouble, or that occasional day we all experience when one's physical reserves are rather lower than normal.

Remember always to ride within your capabilities and do not be over-ambitious in the riding targets which you set. For the novice, a circular route is to be preferred for pleasure jaunts; that way you are never too far from home. And always carry a little money for emergencies.

If the going should get really tough, never be afraid to stop for sustenance. Iron rations of a couple of bars of chocolate or the like should always be carried on any ride of more than thirty miles. The sudden advent of what cyclists call 'the knock'—an extremely unpleasant feeling of nausea and general weakness—can afflict even the fittest cyclist, its root cause being neglect of the inner man. When cycling, always eat before the onset of hunger because, by that time, it will be too late for eating to do much good.

Steep hills present a challenge to one's physique and determination, but it is no sin to get off and walk. If your bike is sensibly geared, few hills should present undue problems but, when there is no hurry, it is often as well to dismount for a while and stretch one's legs. Too many cyclists make a fetish of never being 'beaten', as they put it, by a hill. Well, even the greatest racing men have been known to walk on occasion so there's no disgrace, and what's the sense in deliberately making hard going of it?

Basic physical fitness will of course be of great benefit to the aspiring cyclist, though cycling in itself is the best way of all to achieve such fitness. If your life has latterly been marked by undue physical inactivity, start off with very gentle runs of say three to five miles. Then week by week increase your distances and strike out into tougher territory. Within a month, rides of around fifty miles should be well within the capabilities of even the most sedentary middle-aged businessman who has not engaged in sport since school-days.

Brisk walks, simple exercises like deep-breath-ing and push-ups, and games like tennis and squash are great aids to general fitness. Diet helps too. The cycling athlete needs to follow a pretty strict régime, but the ordinary cyclist can indulge his fancy somewhat more. The art is never to over-indulge. Salads, fruit, fresh fish and meat, green vegetables and wholewheat bread are all admirable, while things like pastries, over-cooked and spicy dishes and too much fried food should as a rule be avoided. All these things may be enjoyed in moderation, however, for the following of a sensible diet should never be turned into a chore of dismal self-denial. Food should be well chewed and eaten slowly. Regular meals should be taken, two big meals a day being preferable to lots of snacks, but remember to allow time for digestion. There is no point in eating a hearty lunch and then jumping straight on the bike to tackle a stiff hill-climb.

Sensible riding dress will also play a part in making your cycling a pleasure. Light clothes, slightly loose-fitting, are the ideal for pleasure cycling, as circulating air trapped in clothing helps to preserve warmth.

Shorts should only be worn in very warm weather (apart from racing) and only then when some warming massage cream has been rubbed into the knees. Creaky joints through unthinking wearing of shorts in wet or cold weather have been the bane of many a cyclist's life.

Pantaloons or plus-twos (like plus-fours but closer cut), together with long cycling socks, are ideal, though there is no reason why you should not ride in long trousers, secured at the ankle with cycle-clips or by the use of quick-release straps to prevent them from snagging the chain.

A good track-suit with close-fitting bottoms is admirable, but, whatever your choice, try to wear something with a good, stout seat (preferably a double seat) or, alternatively, wear a good pair of racing shorts under your trousers, rather than pants—but make sure to wash them each time after use, taking special care of the chamois-leather seat with which they are fitted.

Seams in both under-pants and trousers should not be in the sitting-down area, unless they are of the flush-type, otherwise you will experience

Wearing track suits, tight-fitting plusses, long socks, woollen hats and gloves, this group of racing men is perfectly equipped for winter training miles, and for getting plenty of fun from it

saddle-soreness. In any case, this soreness is something most novices have to endure but it can be alleviated by regular application of surgical spirit to the portions which come in contact with the saddle. This tends to toughen the skin in advance. Should saddle-sores still crop up, treat them with a proprietary product such as Nupercanol which, besides healing the wound, contains a pain-killer.

Proper attention to health and hygiene will help reduce all such problems: keep toe-nails cut short and square; make sure you bath regularly (a rub-down with eau-de-cologne is an invigorating after-ride treatment); dust between your toes with talc; rinse your eyes with an eye-bath after a ride in hot, dusty weather; keep your teeth clean and make regular visits to the dentist—bad teeth can cause digestive

problems which will be heightened at times of strenuous physical exercise.

As for top clothing, wear a T-shirt with a pullover, sweater, casual shirt or racing jersey over the top. In cold weather, a string vest is a good substitute for the T-shirt, as it traps air and preserves warmth.

A wind-proof top sweater or cycling jacket is a good investment, but a sheet of polythene or newspaper stuck up your jersey is an equally effective proofing against cold winter winds. It is a favourite measure effected by racing men, particularly useful when facing a long mountain descent.

If you wear a showerproof jacket or anorak, make sure that the material 'breathes' otherwise you will experience unpleasant perspiration problems.

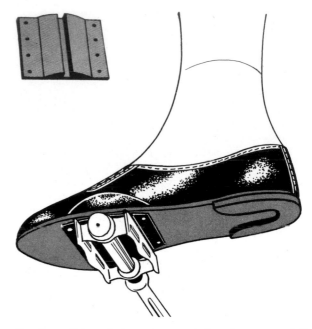

Hands should be protected at all times with track mitts (short-fingered gloves specially developed for cycle racing). These help to avoid blisters and rawness from gripping bars and brake levers on bumpy roads, and also provide protection in a fall. Made with a crochet-type string back, they do not create undue warmth but keep chilliness at bay. In cold weather, substitute a good pair of lined leather or woollen gloves, but make sure that the fingers are not too tight, as this will soon stop efficient blood circulation and lead to cold hands.

The same tip applies to shoes. For general riding, shoes should be of ample fit so as not to impede circulation yet should not allow the foot to slip about too much. Proper cycling shoes are the ideal, but stout-soled sportsman's training shoes or practical lace-up walking shoes will do.

Shallow shoeplates will be a great boon and will not impede walking. They can now be bought in plastic and rubber which obviates the

Tourists will benefit from the use of shoeplates, especially when tackling steep hills, but, to facilitate easy dismounting, they should have a shallower slot than racing types

These bicyclists are taking part in a tourist trial which involves pace judging, map reading and riding technique. Wet weather requires suitable weatherproofing, though the popular poncho-type cape does tend to catch the wind and make steering difficult

66

annoying clip-clop sounds which usually accompanies the cyclist's progress on dismounting.

Wet weather is the one condition that may threaten a cyclist's conviction that he is far better off exercising his limbs in the fresh air than a sedentary motorist is, boxed up in his environment-polluting vehicle and a prey to traffic temper and ulcers. In pouring rain—which may descend without warning to spoil the best-planned rides, and which has to be expected during the winter months by urban utility-riders—a cyclist may be forgiven for envying the motorists who splash by him on the roadway. So always pack some kind of protection against the wet. The simplest is a plastic poncho-shaped cycling cape that drapes over the hands holding the handlebars and covers the handlebar fittings as well. It also keeps the rain off one's knees to a large extent, preventing trousers from becoming soaked. Its disadvantage is that the cape produces wind-resistance, tends to hamper one's control in steering (as one's hands underneath it are not as free for quick movement as normally) and makes out-of-the-saddle work almost impossible. It also has a dangerous tendency to ride up one's back, if it is not tied down properly by an inside tape round the waist, and to blow over one's head. This can obscure one's view of the road behind.

The racing cape, cut like a jacket, is an alternative, but it sets up a perspiration problem and gives no protection to the legs. In this case, use waterproof over-trousers or simple leggings.

As for headgear, well, anything that is practical goes. A beret, a flat cloth-cap, a showerproof golfing cap with peak or the familiar cyclist's racing cap of cotton will all fill the bill by keeping the sun off your head or the rain out of your eyes. In a downpour, a sou'wester may be a useful protection to carry, if any other forms of headgear do not appeal to you for ordinary, fine-weather wear.

A fully-laden tourist fights a gale in the Hebrides. Note how the wind has caused her poncho to ride up at the back

Ideally, cycle clothing should be reasonably close-fitting. Flapping clothes are annoying and create wind drag. This enthusiast is sensibly equipped for cooler weather

Maintenance

The bicycle is a wonderfully resilient piece of machinery, able to take many years of abuse while continuing to give faithful service. However, if you are going to be serious about your cycling then it is as important to keep your cycle fit as it is to keep yourself in good physical trim. A few minutes' attention before and after each ride will bring enormous rewards. A well-maintained machine is a delight, one that is neglected will become sluggish and unreliable in use.

When not in use, your cycle should preferably be kept in a cool, dry place where rust will not attack the metal parts nor heat affect the tyres. There is no need to make a fetish of keeping your cycle clean and sparkling. A quick dust-over after a ride should remove excess dirt, mud and grease, and before going out for a ride in the rain it is a good tip to rub a slightly oily rag over the bright-metal parts, as this will protect them from the damp and can be removed with a quick wipe afterwards. If it becomes drenched without your having taken this precaution, be sure to wipe it dry before putting it away. Give the frame a regular rub over with a clean, dry, soft rag, and it should need no further attention.

Tyres should be kept inflated at the manufacturers' recommended pressures—which usually means very hard—at all times, even when the bike is not in use. This will help to prevent the rubber from cracking and will also lead to safer, easier riding.

Should your tyres wear unevenly, it may mean that your frame is out-of-track, that is to say, slightly twisted, or that the wheel needs truing. In either case, prompt attention is required. Consult a dealer in the former case; with patience you can true a wheel yourself by detecting the loose spokes and tightening them up with a spoke key. Remember, though, that a wheel should not only be free from buckles (side-to-side wavers)—but should also be perfectly circular and have no flat spots. Overtightening the spokes can easily turn a circular wheel into an oval one!

When truing a wheel, spin it gently and hold a piece of chalk just clear of the rim. If it is buckled, the buckled section will lean out and rub against the chalk, which will leave a mark. To correct the buckle, tighten the appropriate spokes on the other side of the buckled section, and this will pull it back into true. Wheel truing is very much a matter of trial and error, but it is an art which can rapidly be acquired even by those who are not especially mechanical by nature.

Before every ride, check your tyres for any small flints or pieces of glass which may have become embedded in the rubber and could work through to cause punctures. Also keep an eye open for worn patches of tread, or for canvas showing through. Check the sidewalls for tears and cuts in the fabric. If a tyre is not A1 then change it at once, and this will most likely save you a lot of inconvenience on the road, and remove the danger of a possibly dangerous blow-out.

When using wired-ons, ensure that the tyre is properly seated on the rim and is not warped. If tubulars are your choice, always fit them carefully, using sufficient tube cement to ensure a firm fit without causing too much mess. A small piece of cigarette paper stuck on the rim opposite the valve hole will give you a starting point for when the time comes to remove the tubular.

Try not to remove tubular tyres too often, as this weakens the fabric and shortens the tyre life, as well as stretching the tyre.

Always carry a spare tubular, unless racing in an event where there are following service vehicles or which is held on a small circuit. In the

Mending a wired-on tyre

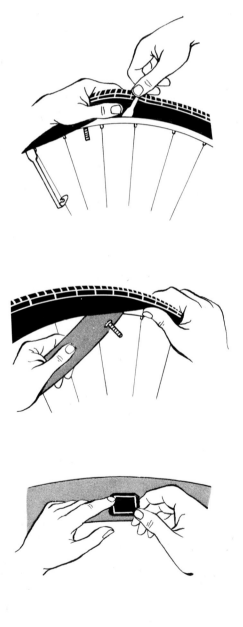

Remove one side of the outer casing from rim with the aid of three tyre-levers, taking care not to nip the inner tube.

Carefully remove the inner tube from the rim and outer casing, taking care not to bend or otherwise damage the valve.
   Inflate inner tube slightly and immerse in a bowl of water (if handy) or hold to ear in order to locate puncture through bubbles or hiss of escaping air.
   Dry tube carefully around the puncture and roughen with fine emery cloth from repair outfit.
   Rub a small amount of rubber solution onto the area adjacent to the puncture and sufficient for affixing suitable sized rubber patch from repair outfit.
   Allow solution to almost dry. Peel backing strip from patch and affix over puncture, taking care that it is not creased and that there are no bubbles in it.

When patch is firmly affixed, dust with French chalk to prevent tube sticking to casing. Check casing for continued presence of foreign objects; patch if necessary or plug hole with tread-stopping compound.
   Replace tube in casing, taking care that neither tube nor rim tape becomes twisted.
Replace outer casing or rim. Do *not* use tyre levers for this process.
   Tyres should be regularly checked for wear and for flints. Faulty valves can be replaced in some makes of inner tube, but a complete new tube is the safer bet.

latter case, you would have little chance of catching up with the field after a puncture, and it will never be too far to walk back to the pit area.

Spare tubulars should always be folded carefully with the tread on the outside, and wrapped in brown paper, an old magazine or cloth to prevent chaffing. Every so often, the spare should be unfolded, and left inflated overnight to prevent it from becoming deformed.

When repairing punctures, take care to dust the patch with french chalk so that excess glue will not stick the tube to the cover.

Light tubulars have very fine inner-tubes which always tend to leak a little and are not too suited to repair by patching. A new tube can be fitted, though, by cutting both old and new tubes, tying the end of the old one to the new one and then pulling the old tube out of the cover which in turn will pull the new one into it. The two ends of the new tube can then be rejoined by rolling one end over the other and affixing with rubber solution. When repairing tubulars, always take care to stitch the covers up evenly as the tyre will otherwise warp.

Repairing tubular tyres

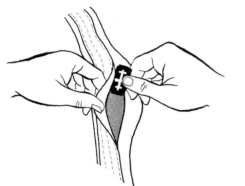

Remove tyre from rim, starting opposite the valve, and using hands only.
Locate puncture by immersing tyre in water or listening for escaping air. The air may, however, be escaping at some distance from the actual puncture in the casing.
Carefully peel back a length of base tape to about three inches on either side of the air leak.

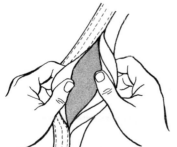

Using a razor blade, with great caution slit base stitching to enable inner tube to be withdrawn.
Repair puncture and outer casing as for wired-on tyres, but using lighter type patches.
Replace inner tube in casing and tuck in chafing tape.
Re-sew, using strong thread, and following line and pattern of original stitch holes.

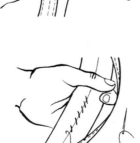

Re-stick base-tape using special cement.
Care should be taken that sufficient rim cement is left on the rim to ensure safe fixing of replaced or replacement tyre.
Spare tubulars should not be kept folded for lengthy periods, as this is liable to cause permanent deformation.

15-speed gearing is achieved by combining a six-speed rear derailleur with a front changer and triple chainrings

Close-up view of a typical rear derailleur mechanism. This Campagnolo model has been drilled out for increased lightness. It can handle up to six sprockets and a very wide gear range

The parts of a bicycle

The points asterisked should be oiled

*1	Quick-release hub mechanism
*2	Large-flange hub
3	Tyre
4	Rim
5	Spoke nipple
6	Spoke
*7	Front brake mechanism (side-pull)
8	Brake hood
9	Brake lever
10	Brake adjuster
*11	Brake cable
12	Handlebar
13	Handlebar stem (or extension)
*14	Head-set
*15	Gear lever
*16	Gear cable
17	Cable clip
18	Saddle
19	Seat-pin
*20	Front changer
21	Toe-strap
22	Toe-clip
*23	Pedal

24	Crank ⎫
25	Chainrings ⎬ Chainset* (bottom bracket axle)
*26	Rear brake mechanism
*27	Rear changer (derailleur gear)
*28	Five-speed block (multiple freewheel)
*29	Chain

Frame parts

A	Head tube
B	Fork crown
C	Fork blade
D	Fork-end
E	Top tube (cross bar)
F	Down tube
G	Seat tube
H	Bottom bracket
I	Seat bolt
J	Brake bridge
K	Seat stay
L	Chain stay
M	Rear drop-out

Wheel hubs will give years of service with little more attention than a regular light oiling of the ball races.

Although many cyclists ride for years without ever doing so, you will find it pays to dismantle your **bottom-bracket** at least once a year and check that the ball-races are not unduly worn or pitted, replace the ball-bearings with new ones, check that the axle is not bent, and then reassemble it, packing with light grease. The same process should be followed with pedals. Especial care should be taken to see that pedal spindles are not bent as this can cause serious harm to the leg muscles. Since you will become used to riding the machine, this twisting may not be noticeable to you in use. The quickest means of detection is to ride another bike that has new pedals. If it gives a strange twisting feeling to your pedalling then you will know that your own pedals need attention.

In this connection, never prop a bike up by the pedals or in such a way that it can fall over onto the pedals, as these are two of the prime causes of bent spindles.

Regularly check the teeth of both chainwheel rings and rear sprockets to see that they have not become hooked or otherwise worn. If they should be worn then replace them immediately,

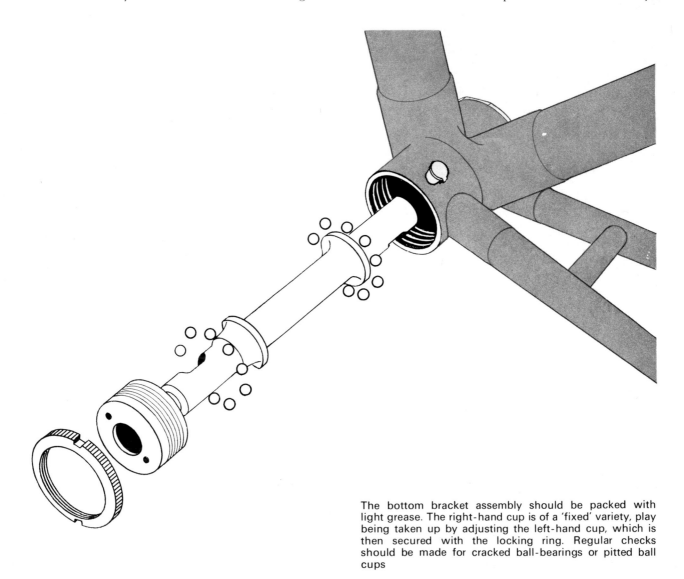

The bottom bracket assembly should be packed with light grease. The right-hand cup is of a 'fixed' variety, play being taken up by adjusting the left-hand cup, which is then secured with the locking ring. Regular checks should be made for cracked ball-bearings or pitted ball cups

as they can lead to chain slip. Similarly, check the **chain** by lifting the links away from the chainwheel teeth. If you can pull them more than an eighth of an inch clear, the chain is stretched and needs replacement.

Never fit a new chain without fitting new sprockets at the same time—and vice versa.

If a chain becomes excessively dirty, it can be cleaned by removing it and leaving it coiled up in a shallow pan of petrol or paraffin. Stubborn particles of grease can be removed with an old toothbrush. After cleaning, the chain should be placed in another pan filled with graphite-based grease or fairly thick lubricating oil. This should

be gently warmed so that the oil will penetrate right in between the links of the chain. After ten minutes, allow the pan to cool, remove the chain and wipe the surplus oil clear.

Your chain should always be kept at the correct tension, which means no more than three-quarters of an inch and no less than half an inch of play on the top run of the chain when the bike is held upright and at rest. Excess slack can be taken up by pulling the wheel further back in the fork-ends on a single-gear or hub-gear machine or by adjusting the chain-tension spring on a derailleur-geared bike.

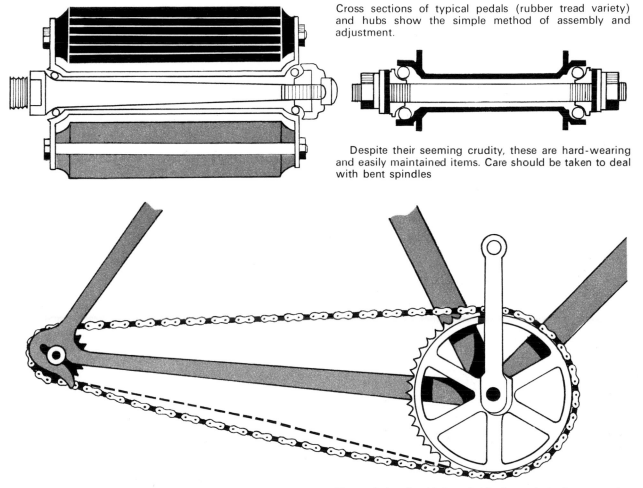

Cross sections of typical pedals (rubber tread variety) and hubs show the simple method of assembly and adjustment.

Despite their seeming crudity, these are hard-wearing and easily maintained items. Care should be taken to deal with bent spindles

Your chain should be checked regularly for excessive play ($\frac{1}{2}$ inch is ideal). A distorted chainring can cause the chain to be too tight in one place, too loose in another. The chain should also be tried for stretch. Either fault can lead to the chain unshipping in use.

Never use a thick oil (such as automobile oil) in a **freewheel** as this will cause the pawl-springs to gum up, so that you freewheel when pedalling in both directions! Dirt can be cleaned off with paraffin or petrol, before re-oiling.

Never be over generous with oil on chain or freewheel as there is a danger of surplus oil running down the spokes, onto the rims and soaking into the tyres and damaging them.

Saddles in plastic need no maintenance. Leather ones should be given an occasional application of neatsfoot oil, Brooks' Proofide, saddle soap or dubbin to the under-side and Proofide to the top in order to keep it in good condition and enable it to 'breathe'. Allow the treatment to soak in thoroughly before using the saddle again, to avoid the possibility of stained clothing.

Any sagging in the top of a leather saddle may be taken up by adjusting the tension screw at the peak of the saddle—but, caution! Never tighten a saddle when it is wet. If a leather saddle squeaks, a light application of oil around the cantle-piece and nose-piece rivets should cure it.

Brakes should always be kept properly adjusted, for your own safety. Make sure the levers are securely fixed to the handlebars and will not move. Regularly take the cables out of their casings and, if frayed, replace them. The cables should also be kept lightly oiled, as should the moving parts of the brake mechanism itself.

I find it best to allow a fair amount of movement in the brakes before they come into action. This means that, should you buckle a wheel, the brakes will not foul it. Moreover, it also leads to a smoother braking action with less danger of snatch. One more good reason: in an emergency you are likely to grab at your brakes as a reflex

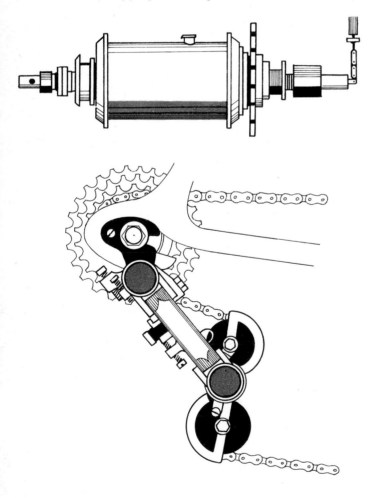

The hub gear **left** is totally encased against the weather but is heavy, complicated in construction, difficult to repair and liable to slip in use. Derailleur gears **below left** are lighter, simpler and easier to maintain but more susceptible to damage, causing greater chain wear and being adversely affected by such wear

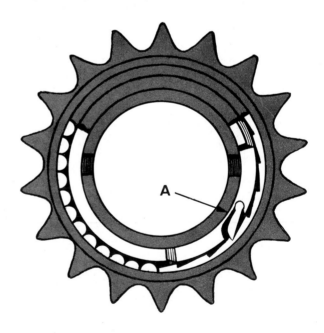

The sectional view of a freewheel **above** clearly shows the pawl **A** engaging a spline. Use of excessively thick oil will jam the pawl, causing its unfortunate owner to freewheel in both directions

action, and this can lead to a skid if you have your brakes adjusted too close to the rims.

On the other hand, ensure that full braking action is available well before the lever comes close to the bars. If you are able to pull the lever till it touches the bars then your brakes are dangerously slack.

Handlebars should be tight in the stem and the stem so tight in the forks that you cannot twist the bars when standing with your legs gripping the front-wheel and both hands pulling at the bars with normal force. If the stem moves, tighten the expander bolt.

There should be no slack in your headset as this will lead to poor steering and cause a shuddering effect when braking. Whilst talking of braking—remember the front brake is most powerful but is likely to send you over the bars, while over-application of the back brake will cause skidding. Try to apply both brakes with equal force and with a gentle but firm, rather than a sudden snatching movement.

Multiple gears should be kept carefully adjusted according to the makers' instructions and should neither unship the chain from the sprockets or chainrings nor go into the spokes. Simple adjusting screws are fitted to take care of this. Check for excessive play in the gear mechanisms, as this will cause poor changes. Twisted gear mechanisms will have the same effect and should be replaced.

Gear rollers require only light oiling and check for wear—make sure they revolve freely as otherwise they will cause chain wear.

A once-weekly check of all bolts and screws, regular oiling and cleaning will ensure that your cycle gives many years of reliable service, and will save expensive repair bills.

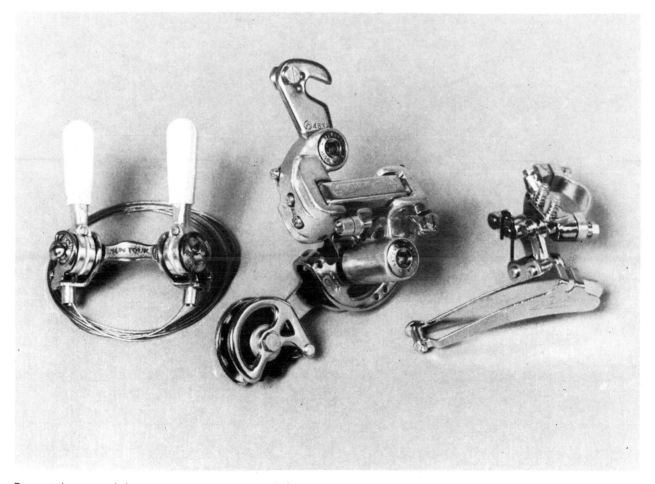

Down-tube control levers, rear mechanism and front changer of a typical derailleur gear set-up capable of providing 8, 10, 12 or even 18 gears. (Five rear sprockets plus double chainring 5 × 2 = 10 gears; six rear sprockets plus triple chainring 6 × 3 = 18)

Touring

There can be few holidays which match the sheer joyfulness of cycle touring. You are your own master, the highway stretches on invitingly you have a fair speed at your disposal yet you remain in close touch with nature. You are able to hear the whistling of the birds, smell the clean-scented country air, sneak up on wild life and actually see animals of which the motorist can only read in books. You will find it easier to meet local people, too, as they are often eager to pass a cheery word with one who so obviously derives pleasure from the countryside without bringing noise and pollution to it. Somehow the view from the top of a great mountain pass looks better when you have reached those lofty heights through your own efforts, and even mundane scenery takes on a new dimension when viewed from a bicycle saddle.

You can stop as and when you like. There is no parking problem. When stopping to do a spot of

sight-seeing, remember to lock your cycle to deter would-be thieves. It is not much use simply chaining the rear-wheel to the frame-stays, for it is relatively easy to carry away a bike. You should chain it to stout railings or a lamp-post, passing the chain of the lock around both frame-tubes and back-wheel spokes.

Having said all this, it must be admitted that a cycle tour can degenerate into a disheartening experience if you do not plan it carefully. Most important of all, do not be over-ambitious. Set yourself modest daily targets. These can always be extended should the going prove easier than you expected. I would say that fifty or sixty miles a day is ideal, and less in mountainous country.

A method I have often followed is to set off at around 10 am so as to arrive at my destination in the early afternoon, after stopping *en route* for lunch. Then, after finding accommodation and

In the back-of-beyond, the bicyclist really comes into his own. **Middle** Governor Ed Whitcomb of Indiana (second from left) and his wife Pat leads a 'Huff-'n-Puff' tour of the Lincoln Trail in Illinois

unloading my luggage, I am free to explore the surrounding district unencumbered. If you are booking accommodation, you can afford to arrive at your chosen accommodation later in the day. On the other hand, there is nothing worse than knowing that you simply have to reach the chosen town, with another twenty or thirty more miles to cover in pouring rain and night fast descending. Should you decide not to book in advance, then always seek out accommodation as early as possible, allowing enough time in hand to cover further miles should you be unable to find anywhere to stay in the district.

Planning points

First, make sure to join one of the cycling associations which provide touring services, such as the Cyclists Touring Club and British Cycling Federation in Great Britain and the League of American Wheelmen and International Touring Society in the United States. Besides providing protection in the form of special third-party and personal accident insurances, they will help you to plan a tour by offering advice on the area you intend to visit, furnishing maps and recommended accommodation and catering addresses, details of road conditions, tourist attractions and so on. The CTC also publish a useful magazine, 'Cycle Touring', which is free to members. The British weekly publication 'Cycling' also includes much touring advice as well as covering racing. France has several specialised cycle-touring publications.

The CTC and the Youth Hostels Association in Britain and the American Youth Hostels and International Touring Society in the USA actually organise guided cycle tours of varying lengths and toughness, both in their own countries and abroad. These range from flat, leisurely 15-miles-a-day rambles to ambitious 100-miles-a-day trips in arduous conditions. These are an ideal grounding for any aspiring cycle tourist, enabling one to assimilate the experience gained by the tour leaders over many years of cycling.

Let us now consider the bike you are going to use, whether it is a specialised touring mount,

your everyday cycle with luggage added, or your racing machine suitably adapted. Before embarking on any trip away from home, ensure that your tyres are free from cuts, the gears and brakes function properly, wheels are 'true' and the moving parts are well lubricated.

Adapt your riding position. For comfortable touring, you can afford to sit lower, with the bars slightly higher than for speed work. Gearing will also need consideration. The gears that seem ideal when you are racing will not be right when your bike is loaded down with touring kit. The same applies to the utility bike, which is normally ridden in a fairly uncluttered condition.

For touring in undulating country you will need a bottom gear of around 45 inches (see gear-chart), while for mountain work you can go much lower. On the other hand, while an occasional burst of speed downhill can be most

Gear table

Sprocket	38		40		42		44		45		46		47		48		49		50		51		52		53		54		55		56	
Wheel Size	26"	27"	26"	27"	26"	27"	26"	27"	26"	27"	26"	27"	26"	27"	26"	27"	26"	27"	26"	27"	26"	27"	26"	27"	26"	27"	26"	27"	26"	27"	26"	27"
12	82.4	85.5	86.7	90.0	91.0	94.5	95.3	99.0	97.5	101.2	99.7	103.5	101.8	105.7	104.0	108.0	106.1	110.2	108.3	112.5	110.5	114.7	112.7	117.0	114.8	119.3	117.0	121.5	119.1	123.7	121.3	126.0
13	76.0	78.9	80.0	83.1	84.0	87.2	88.0	91.4	90.0	93.4	92.0	95.5	94.0	97.6	96.0	99.7	98.0	101.8	100.0	103.9	102.0	105.9	104.0	108.0	106.0	110.0	108.0	112.1	110.0	114.2	112.0	116.3
14	70.6	73.3	74.3	77.1	78.0	81.0	81.7	84.9	83.5	86.8	85.4	88.7	87.3	90.6	89.1	92.6	91.0	94.5	92.9	96.4	94.7	98.3	96.6	100.3	98.4	102.2	100.3	104.1	102.1	106.0	104.0	108.0
15	65.9	68.4	69.3	72.0	72.8	75.6	76.3	79.2	78.0	81.0	79.7	82.8	81.5	84.6	83.2	86.4	84.9	88.2	86.7	90.0	88.4	91.8	90.1	93.6	91.9	95.4	93.6	97.2	95.3	99.0	97.0	100.8
16	61.8	64.1	65.0	67.5	68.3	70.9	71.5	74.3	73.1	75.9	74.6	77.6	76.4	79.3	78.0	81.0	79.6	82.7	81.3	84.4	82.9	86.0	84.5	87.8	86.1	89.4	87.7	91.1	89.3	92.8	91.0	94.5
17	58.1	60.3	61.2	63.5	64.2	66.7	67.3	69.9	68.9	71.5	70.4	73.1	71.9	74.6	73.4	76.2	74.9	77.8	76.5	79.4	78.0	81.0	79.5	82.6	81.0	84.1	82.5	85.7	84.1	87.3	85.6	88.9
18	54.9	57.0	57.8	60.0	60.6	63.0	63.6	66.0	65.0	67.5	66.4	69.0	67.9	70.5	69.3	72.0	70.7	73.5	72.2	75.0	73.6	76.5	75.1	78.0	76.5	79.5	78.0	81.0	79.4	82.5	80.8	84.0
19	52.0	54.0	54.7	56.8	57.5	59.7	60.2	62.5	61.6	64.0	62.9	65.4	64.3	66.8	65.7	68.2	67.0	69.6	68.4	71.1	69.8	72.4	71.2	73.9	72.5	75.3	73.9	76.7	75.2	78.1	76.6	79.5
20	49.4	51.3	52.0	54.0	54.6	56.7	57.2	59.4	58.5	60.7	59.8	62.1	61.1	63.4	62.4	64.8	63.7	66.2	65.0	67.5	66.3	68.9	67.6	70.2	68.9	71.5	70.2	72.9	71.5	74.3	72.8	75.6
21	47.1	48.9	49.5	51.4	52.0	54.0	54.5	56.6	55.7	57.9	57.0	59.1	58.2	60.4	59.4	61.7	60.7	63.0	61.9	64.3	63.1	65.6	64.4	66.9	65.6	68.1	66.9	69.4	68.1	70.7	69.3	72.0
22	44.9	46.6	47.3	49.1	49.6	51.5	52.0	54.0	53.2	55.2	54.4	56.5	55.5	57.7	56.7	58.9	57.9	60.1	59.1	61.4	60.3	62.6	61.5	63.8	62.6	65.0	63.8	66.3	65.0	67.5	66.2	68.7
23	43.0	44.6	45.2	47.0	47.5	49.3	49.7	51.6	50.9	52.8	52.0	54.0	53.1	55.2	54.3	56.3	55.4	57.5	56.5	58.7	57.6	59.9	58.8	61.0	59.9	62.2	61.0	63.4	62.2	64.6	63.3	65.7
24	41.2	42.8	43.3	45.0	45.5	47.3	47.7	49.5	48.8	50.6	49.8	51.8	50.9	52.9	52.0	54.0	53.1	55.1	54.2	56.3	55.3	57.4	56.3	58.5	57.4	59.6	58.5	60.8	59.6	61.9	60.7	63.0
25	39.5	41.0	41.6	43.2	43.7	45.4	45.8	47.5	46.8	48.6	47.8	49.7	48.9	50.8	49.9	51.8	51.0	52.9	52.0	54.0	53.0	55.1	54.1	56.2	55.1	57.2	56.2	58.3	57.2	59.4	58.2	60.5
26	38.0	39.5	40.0	41.5	42.0	43.6	44.0	45.7	45.0	46.7	46.0	47.8	47.0	48.8	48.0	49.8	49.0	50.9	50.0	51.9	51.0	53.0	52.0	54.0	53.0	55.0	54.0	56.1	55.0	57.1	56.0	58.2
28	35.3	36.6	37.1	38.6	39.0	40.5	40.9	42.4	41.8	43.4	42.7	44.4	43.6	45.3	44.6	46.3	45.5	47.2	46.4	48.2	47.4	49.2	48.3	50.1	49.2	51.1	50.1	52.1	51.1	53.0	52.0	54.0

Any gear ratio that is not shown in the table **left** can be calculated as follows:

$$\text{gear} = \frac{\text{number of teeth on chain wheel}}{\text{number of teeth on sprocket}} \times \text{diameter of rear wheel in inches}$$

---

exhilarating, you will not really need a top gear above 95 to 100 inches.

For touring with fairly heavy loads, a free-wheel block of 14, 16, 19, 23, 28 with front chainrings of 34–50 will enable most terrains to be conquered; anything much lower is pretty useless and you might as well get off and walk. The use of 15-speed gearing allows 'reserve' extra low gears to be available. However, hard-riding tourists will tend to gear somewhat higher than this and may in fact favour closer ratios. Many British enthusiasts used to tour on a single fixed-gear of 69 inches before multi-speed gearing became universally popular, though this certainly made for tough work.

All your luggage should be carried on the bike and not on your person. After all, the bicycle is a most willing workhorse, so why burden yourself with clumsy shoulder-packs and accompanying aches and strains? The familiar saddlebag is the popular way of carrying luggage among British riders, but the Continentals have a far better idea. They keep weight low, and the bicycle far easier to handle, by fitting rear pannier-type carriers. Take care, though, that these do not foul your ankles when pedalling.

For heavier loads, small handlebar bags and front panniers are added by our European friends, and for the still heavier loads required by cycle-camping they sometimes tow a simple one-wheeled trailer, though I personally would not fancy such an encumbrance. Touring bags should be attached by easy-to-use quick-release fittings and should ideally be waterproof. If they are not, then line them with plastic bags to keep your spare clothing dry.

The problem with touring is not so much in deciding what to take as what to leave behind.

Sturdy, well-chosen panniers and saddlebag will carry enough luggage for a truly independent holiday. Bicycle camping has many adherents, while others prefer to rely on youth hostels or hotels

Through tourist trials, map-reading contests and paper-trails, the hard-riding tourist can add an element of competition to his bicycling. This rider is taking part in the British Cycle Tourist Competition

Never overburden yourself, but take sufficient to ensure your comfort even if it turns out to be a rain-sodden trip. Take spare socks, spare underwear, a spare sweater and, perhaps, an easily washed drip-dry shirt for evening wear and spare trousers (of a type which can double for evening wear and for riding). Sturdy 'stay-pressed' trousers or corduroy jeans are ideal, but denim jeans should be avoided as they do not preserve warmth when wet. A pair of basketball boots or training shoes take up little space and can, if needed, double as riding shoes. You will need toothbrush, shaving kit and towel, soap and flannel, of course.

Some weight can be saved by posting a parcel of clean clothing to be called for at a post office *en-route*. To my mind, the best idea of all is to have a motor vehicle accompanying the tour. It need not necessarily follow your route, although some organised group tours often arrange for a vehicle to do so, but can simply be a car driven by friends or family who are taking a motoring holiday in the same area. It is a simple matter to arrange to link up each evening. In that way you only need to carry your requirements for the day, while the vehicle can transport changes of clothing and spare wheels, suits for evening use and so on.

If, however, you are touring entirely on your own, then make sure that you have a tool-kit sufficient to meet most contingencies. This should include a screwdriver, a spoke key for tightening or replacing wheel spokes and a range of spanners (a small adjustable spanner plus one of the eight-holed cyclists' spanners will suffice). Some people carry things like chain removers, oilers, spare spindles, and a welter of other equipment so that they resemble a mobile workshop, but this is not really necessary unless one is touring in a particularly remote region. Even then, replacement parts can if necessary be phoned for and sent by return post. One tourist who snapped a crank in the wilderness of the Scottish Highlands obtained a replacement all the way from London, 450 miles to the south, within two days.

However, a couple of spare spokes, a spare chain-link, spare bulbs, a puncture repair outfit and a spare inner-tube (if using 'wired-ons') or two or three spare tyres (if using tubulars) together with a basic first-aid kit are worth the extra weight involved. Useful, too, are little gadgets like a map measure and a small compass, while most tourists will want to carry a camera, in which case a 35mm job is the obvious ideal, being very convenient in size and not unduly heavy.

Many good maps are available in sizes ideal for cyclists (the Michelin one centimetre to two kilometres in Europe and the Ordnance Survey one-inch to the mile and Bartholomew's half-inch to the mile in Britain, for instance). Choose one which shows contours or at least gives road gradients—otherwise you might be in for some unpleasant shocks when confronted by unanticipated upgrades.

A very useful item is a small plaque or ticket attached to your bike, giving your name and home address (plus possibly an address in the country you are visiting), just in case the bike should be mislaid when being transported by train, boat or plane. The Bicycle Riders Association in America offer a computerised 'cycle registration' service to deter thieves.

When touring abroad, make sure that your passport is in order and that you have the necessary visas. Some countries require special documentation for your cycle, and bodies like the CTC can advise you on this.

As for choosing an area—well, that is very much a matter of personal taste, but again the various touring bodies can advise and in some instances will even sell you the necessary travel tickets and make reservations for you.

One of the most convenient ways of reaching your chosen touring area is, of course, by automobile and there are now several specially-adapted roof-racks and trailers on the market which make transportation of three, four or even five cycles simplicity itself.

As for meals and accommodation, you may prefer the comfort of restaurants and hotels or the simplicity of picnics and camping. But

Even a flat tyre can bring light-hearted moments once you are in the great outdoors

Snow and ice are little handicap for the enthusiast.
For once the tricyclist is at an advantage, thanks to his
machine's greater stability in such conditions

With the aid of a roof-rack or trailer, a car can be used
to reach far-off touring or racing areas

More than 500 bicyclists took part in the 1971 Great Western Bicycling Rally in Del Mar, California

whatever you do, prepare for emergencies. At least one plastic feeding-bottle should be carried on the bike, and be topped up each morning. You should also carry emergency rations in the form of a few sandwiches or a chocolate bar.

In Britain, the CTC and BCF both issue lists of recommended caterers and people providing accommodation for cyclists; the American organisations provide similar touring advice. In France the 'Les Routiers' (which cater primarily for long-distance truck drivers) offer good wholesome food and clean beds at reasonable prices.

If you are picknicking, take care not to leave litter behind, and, should you prefer to brew-up over a primus stove (special models are available for carrying on bikes) or an open fire, then make absolutely sure that you do so where it is safe to do so, and *put the fire out properly afterwards.*

Youth hostels offer cheap and agreeable accommodation, and an element of companionship with other lovers of the outdoor life. Most countries now have a web of such hostels, but these can vary enormously in standards from the frankly primitive to the positively luxurious. Find out the details in advance. Camping is a further alternative but does have the disadvantage of greatly increasing the baggage to be carried. If it should be your choice, go for a simple, lightweight one-piece tent with built-in groundsheet, and invest in a good-quality, kapok-filled sleeping bag. Having spent nights out under the stars or simply in a barn, as well as under canvas, I can vouch for the value of such an item which will be sure to keep you snug and warm.

You will need to pay special attention to your pannier carriers when camping. Make sure that they are sturdy enough to support the extra weight, and that they do not sway about, as this will produce dangerous wobbling when riding.

Choose a good site when pitching your tent, preferably on rising ground, close enough to a hedge or woods to provide a wind-break but not actually under trees as they will both keep the sun off and drip moisture onto the tent as well as making a dangerous spot in an electric storm. Do not camp too close to water either, as sudden

The ultimate in long-distance cycling? British singer and cycling enthusiast 'Big Pete' Duker rode round the world during 1971 and *en route* set a new record for the American crossing from Los Angeles to New York. Cool water brings relief to hot feet in the New Mexico desert

rainfall can make a river or pool suddenly over-flow its banks. What is more, midges, gnats and other insect pests are likely to be encountered near water.

Before pitching camp, make sure you have asked for permission. It is vital to foster good relationships with those who live and work in the country, not for your sake alone but for all other visitors.

With proper forethought, cycle touring is a wonderful experience. You have greater range than the walker, yet you get close to nature in a way that those cocooned inside the glass cages of their cars never do.

Mountains, deserts, roads, bridle paths, disused railways, even seaside beaches feel the wheel-marks of explorative cyclists

From eight to eighty, the pleasures of cycling in good company are there for everyone to enjoy

Bicycling for pleasure in all seasons and places
. . . in the hills of Spain **top left**, in an English winter
top right and with a club in the heat of southern
California **bottom** . . . through unspoiled woodland **top**
and across a Scottish burn **bottom**

Racing

Within the three main divisions of road-racing, time-trialling and track-racing there are many sub-divisions, each of which produces its specialists, though most racing cyclists tend to mix their racing quite a lot, either because there simply aren't enough events available to them in their chosen branch of the sport or because they prefer some variety in their racing. Most fit riders can adapt themselves admirably to almost any branch of racing though it is true that each tends to favour a different type of competitor, sprinters usually being big-built, climbers tending to be lean and wiry.

Road Racing

Single day events

The most popular form of cycle-racing is the one-day road-race. This event can be infinitely varied in nature, depending on the type of course used. It can be a large circuit, a small one, a place-to-place course or an out-and-back one over roads hilly or flat and covering any distance from ten to two hundred miles. Most amateur single-day races are of between fifty and one hundred miles in length, while professionals usually race over distances from eighty to one hundred and eighty miles. The world championship distance is usually around one hundred and forty miles for amateurs and one hundred and eighty for the professionals.

Road races are held on the massed-start principle, first man over the finishing line being the winner, though some circuit races are decided on a points basis, these points being awarded to the first riders across the line on each lap.

Subsidiary prizes are often awarded for special sprints, or 'primes' as they are known, *en route*. These may be on the summit of a hill, passing through a town or at the finishing point of the circuit, or some other vantage spot.

When such races are held on very small circuits they are often known as criterium or kermesse races, and these events form the backbone of the sport and provide the best spectator attraction, in that the riders pass by every few minutes, though this may not compare with the greater glamour of the personalities in the great place-to-place classics.

Stage racing

Stage races are road events run in stages, with the winner being the rider with the shortest aggregate time over all the stages, after deduction of any bonuses for stage placings. Each stage is run like a separate race, with the riders starting in one group. At the end of a stage, the time taken by each man is added to his time for the earlier stages, in order to calculate his standing on the general classification.

These races are usually of several days' or even weeks' duration, but sometimes a single-day event may be split into stages.

Professional racing is highly sophisticated with teams sponsored by major industrial concerns and provided with specially-adapted service cars

A team-mate gives up his rear-wheel for puncture victim Raymond Poulidor, one of the great French champions

Centre Even the toughest professionals sometimes find the going too tough. French ace Joseph Groussard topples over backwards on the Mur de Surmano, 1961
Bottom Three all-time greats: Britain's late Tom Simpson, leads Belgium's Rik Van Looy and Germany's Rudi Altig

In most stage races, a special leader's jersey is awarded at the start of the stage to the rider leading overall and he wears it for that stage. The previous year's winner, if riding, usually wears the jersey on the opening stage. This now famous idea was first introduced in the 1919 Tour de France, when one of the team managers, Alphonse Bauge, suggested to the Tour's founder, Henri Desgrange, that some mark of distinction should be provided so that the public could pick out the race leader in the bunch. Since Desgrange's newspaper, 'L'Auto', was printed on yellow paper, this colour was chosen. In the same way, the Giro d'Italia later adopted pink.

Since 1947, the initials 'HD' have been embroidered on the Tour's yellow jersey in memory of Desgrange.

Desgrange, a former world one-hour record-holder on the track, founded the Tour de France, the greatest race of them all, in 1903, when victory went to Maurice Garin. Since then it has produced many of the most remarkable exploits of cycling. Apart from anything else, it is the world's longest cycle race.

The longest single-stage race ever run was the 750 mile Paris-Brest-Paris—so tough that it was only run every 10 years. The first occasion was won by Charles Terront of France in 1891 at an average speed of 15 mph. At the other end of the scale, the fastest-ever classic was the Paris-Roubaix of 1964 won by Peter Post of Holland at an average of nearly 30 mph.

France's Jean Robic, winner of the 1947 Tour de France, sports the goggles, double bottle cages and other impedimenta of his era. Note the two spare tubular tyres

If modern roadman Yves Hezard, also of France, gets a flat tyre, a service car will give him a rapid wheel change. Improved roads obviate the need for heavy equipment and goggles

High on an Alpine pass, the gruelling Tour de France swaps the heat of the midsummer plains for snowlined roads

Australian pursuit road-race

This is the name given to road-races run on a handicap formula, almost all Australian events being conducted this way. The most famous is Warnambool-Melbourne (nearly 200 miles) in which the scratch-men often concede more than an hour's handicap to the long-markers.

Time Trialling

In a time-trial, each rider is timed separately over the ordained distance. Riders are dispatched at regular intervals (usually of one minute in England, three minutes on the Continent) and each rider must cover the distance alone and unpaced. If another rider is overtaken, it is forbidden for the two to keep company, the caught rider being required to keep clear of the overtaker.

In Britain, this remains the major sector of cycling sport. As with road racing, the season gets under way towards the end of February and tails off in October, when specialised hill-climb events are held. These are simply a time-trial up a suitable hill or mountain, and one of the most arduous forms of cycle competition.

Events in Britain are usually held over set distances or times (10 miles, 25 miles, 30 miles, 50 miles or 100 miles; 12 hours or 24 hours). All courses are accurately measured and since there

The Tour of Britain Milk Race is British cycling's top event, though only open to amateurs, and draws riders from many nations

are coveted national records at each distance the most popular events are those held on the fastest courses. These are usually those which have a good surface, few corners, gentle undulations (surprisingly, this is faster than a dead-flat road) and carry heavy traffic. Traffic sets up an air drag and creates the controversial 'suck-and-blow' effect which has caused many critics to question the worth of times set on such courses. The 25-mile record is now approaching the sub-50 minute standard while over 500 miles have been covered in 24 hours.

In other countries, time trials are usually held on more sporting courses, usually on one or two laps of a circuit with hills, corners and rough roads thrown in for good measure. Such events are a far better test of a rider's skill and strength, as top British time-trialists have found to their cost when visiting such Continental events as the Grand Prix des Nations in France.

Team time-trialling
In this event, which otherwise is the same as the solo time-trial, riders are grouped into teams of anything from two to ten riders. The riders in a team share the pace with each other, but are not allowed to take pace from other teams.

The top event in this sphere is the professional Baracchi Trophy race held in Northern Italy at the end of each season and contested by two-man teams, while in the amateur ranks both world and Olympic titles are awarded over a 100-kilometre distance and with four-man teams.

Track Racing

Cycle racing tracks vary from the super-fast, steeply-banked wooden board tracks such as the Vigorelli in Milan and the Mexico and Munich Olympic tracks, to bumpy grass ovals. Grass track racing, once extremely popular in Britain

A well-drilled Italian squad caught in action during a world team-trial championship. Each rider takes turns at making the pace

Where no specially built banked hard track exists, a grass
oval makes a handy substitute and furnishes exciting if
somewhat slower racing

Time-trialling, the 'race of truth' where each man
competes alone against the clock. In Continental races,
riders like Gösta Petterson of Sweden, in action here,
have the advantage of a following vehicle

The winter cross-country race of cyclo-cross is among
the toughest forms of cycling competition, involving
running and jumping over obstacles. British star Keith
Mernickle has won more than a hundred such races

and still so in the West Indies, New Zealand and
South Africa, demands special skills, tracks
being unbanked; the same applies to cinder
tracks.

Most venues today, however, are of the 'hard-
track' variety, with surfaces of tarmac, concrete
or wood and with banked bends of varying
steepness. The smaller the track, the steeper the
bankings—all in the aid of sustained speed.

Some tracks are as large as 600 metres and
some of the Continental indoor tracks are as
small as 150 metres, but the most usual sizes are
between 300 and 400 metres for outdoor tracks
and around 200 metres for indoor tracks.

Britain has some dozen tracks in regular use,
the United States almost as many, while the

Bicycle speedway on small cinder tracks is full of thrills
and spills. Note the special machines

94

Some of bicycle-racing's most thrilling moments are found during the changes of a madison chase. The madison is a form of relay race usually held on steeply banked indoor tracks

Continent has very many more, though these tend to be far less frequently used, some only staging one meeting a year. London's Paddington track, on the other hand, has racing at least two nights a week, catering for nearly 200 riders.

Most indoor tracks are temporary constructions, put up only for an annual six-day race, usually in an exhibition hall or similar building.

Sprinting

This is the classic form of track racing, the 'Blue Riband' of cycling.

Grand Prix and championship racing is held on the match race principle, involving only two or three riders per race, with the competition

Compare the single fixed-gear, no-brakes track racing machine **left** with the 12-gear road racing bike **right**, each purpose-designed for its event

Holland's 'king of the board tracks', Peter Post, who retired with more than 40 six-day race victories to his credit (a world record), gives a madison hand-sling to partner Patrick Sercus of Belgium

Bicycling's Blue Riband event, the match sprint calls for sophisticated tactics. Here Australia's Gordon Johnson and Italy's Carlo Rancati 'stand still' in an attempt to force each other to take the lead

on a knockout basis, beaten riders getting a chance to win their way back into the next round via 'repèchage' or second-chance races.

In the final rounds, such racing is held on a best of three basis. These events are held over the 1000 metres distance, but since only the last 200 metres are timed, the first part of the race is usually a battle of nerves and wits, each rider trying either to force his rival to take up the front-running position or to spring a surprise by launching a sudden attack when the other man is off guard. Riders may even come to an actual standstill, balancing with great skill in an attempt to force the other man to the front since the back-runner holds the element of surprise. Many tactical wiles are employed, bewildering to the first-time onlooker but a joy to the connoisseur.

In less important races, any number of riders —even a dozen or more—may be put up in each heat. This can lead to more spectacular racing, but gives less scope for tactical riding, as it generally turns into a hell-for-leather affair.

Pursuiting

In a pursuit race, two men are matched against each other, starting in the same direction but at opposite sides of the track. These races are usually held over four or five thousand metres or for a duration of ten minutes. The idea is for each rider to try to catch his rival within the distance. This, in fact, rarely happens, so most races are decided on the rider who covers the distance in the shortest time.

A station pursuit is one where anything up to eight riders are on the track, spaced out equally. Any rider caught within the distance by another is eliminated.

Team pursuiting follows the same principles, but with teams instead of individuals. In world championship racing there are teams of four, the time of the third finisher in each team counting. Each rider in a team will take a lap or half-lap spell at the front, making the pace, then swing up the bank to drop down on the tail of the string until it is again his turn at the front. In an Italian team pursuit, the leading man drops off each team at the end of every lap, until only two men are left to fight it out.

Riders in each four-man squad share the pace during a
team pursuit race. The man up the banking is dropping
back after his turn at the front

Handicap Races

These can be of almost any distance and the
riders are allowed so many metres start over the
scratchman, in accordance with ability shown
in previous races. In Denmark, where there is
tote betting on races, the handicap is very
popular, as it also is in Australia.

Scratch races

A race of any distance in which all competitors
start together. Three, five and ten miles and
twenty kilometres are the popular distances.

Devil-take-the-hindmost

Known as the 'elimination' in France and the
'miss and out' in Australia, this colourfully-
named race is one in which the last rider (or
in some races, the last two) to cross the line on
each lap is eliminated, until a predetermined
number of riders remain to fight the final sprint.
Sometimes as many as six or eight may be left,
but often the race is whittled down to just two
men. This leads to much spectacular and tightly-
bunched sprinting, the interest of each lap
being at the tail rather than the head of the field.

Paced racing

Paced racing involves the use of motor-cycles
(or formerly tandems or triplets, or even teams
of solo riders), which set the pace for their man
while he stays as close as possible to the pacer's
rear wheel in order to gain the optimum shelter
from the wind. The motor-cycles are often
fitted with small rollers projecting at the rear
which reduce the risk of crashes should the
follower ride too close and come into contact.
Speeds of 60 mph are often attained in motor-
paced racing.

Very popular on the small indoor tracks is
Derny-paced racing. This involves the use of a
motor-assisted pacing bicycle (known as a
Derny) fitted with a very high-geared fixed
wheel. The pacer gains extra speed, and also
ensures a smooth pace, by pedalling constantly.

The fastest speed ever attained by a cyclist
behind pace was an incredible 126 mph set up
by 46-year-old Frenchman José Meiffret when
paced by a Mercedes 300 SLR sports car fitted
with a giant windshield. The successful ride
was carried out on a German autobahn in 1951,
Meiffret having earlier crashed at a speed in

High-revving 'Derny' pacing bikes provide some thrilling moments during six-day races, where they are used in subsidiary events to the main madison

Battling against gravity, the hill-climber comes to the end of a short but highly fatiguing effort in this speciality event

The big motors present a hair-raising spectacle as they scorch round at speeds of 50–60 mph, while the pace-followers seek optimum wind shelter

excess of 100 mph.

Meiffret's ride—and the previous record set in the States by Belgian rider, Alfred Letournier—were in the nature of dare-devil feats. More of an athletic achievement was the $76\frac{1}{4}$ miles covered in the hour by Léon Vanderstuyft of Belgium at Montlehery near Paris before the war.

Unknown distance

In this event riders are not told the distance they have to cover, the first warning they get being the bell which signifies the start of the last lap. Something of a lottery in sporting terms, this nevertheless leads to some spirited and crowd-pleasing riding.

Point-to-point

Rather than the winner of the last lap taking the race, that honour goes to the rider who amasses the most points in various intermediate sprints, usually the final lap counts for double points.

Courses des primes

This is a race in which most of the prizes go to winners of various sprints held throughout the race either every lap, every other lap or every five laps.

Madison

In the early days, six-day races were held in which riders literally rode for six days and nights, the first (held in 1896) being won by England's Teddy Hale, who covered 1920 miles in the 144 hours of racing. A year later, American ace Miller logged 2018 miles. He also covered 1411 miles to win a hundred-hour event. But these were inhuman races. After Miller had won at San Francisco in 1899, with a stupendous tally of 2125 miles, he had to be literally wrested from his machine, as he was by then riding on and on like an automaton. Even when they finally put him to bed, his legs still kept up a circling motion!

Such was the public outcry and the official hostility to such events that the New York promoters hit on the idea of making things easier by running a six-day race as a kind of relay race, with two-man teams.

That first two-man six at Madison Square Gardens saw a victory for Miller and his compatriot Waller and this type of relay racing has ever since been known as the Madison, or, to the French, the 'Américaine'.

1973 brought the once popular six-day races back to America. In pre-war years, they rated alongside the World Series as sporting spectacles. Here Mayor La Guardia starts the 1937 New York event

Hand-slinging during a madison. Gerben Karstens,
below, throws his Dutch compatriot and team-mate
Leo Duyndam into the fray

London's Skol Six-Day track at Wembley illustrates a
typical indoor venue, the bowl being banked at nearly
60° in the bends and only 160 metres around

Over the years, six-day races have been cut in severity until, today, riders only have to race for a few hours each evening and can spend the rest of the time relaxing and recovering their reserves of speed. Until quite recently, however, one man from each team still had to continue slowly circling the track during what was known as the neutralisation period.

Few races are as thrilling as a top-class six-day, even though there is quite a bit of showmanship involved and some soft-pedalling to ensure that the top men do not just ride away from the rest and turn the whole thing into a boring procession.

At one time, every major American city had its 'six', as many European cities do now, but unfortunately this type of racing went into an eclipse in America during the 1930s and has yet to recover, though several wealthy businessmen have recently expressed an interest in bringing its thrills back to American audiences.

During a Madison, each member of the team takes one or two laps in the race and then hands over to his comrade by throwing him into the chase with a hefty tug at his shorts or by a hand-sling (the latter is banned in amateur racing, however). These Madison changes are highly spectacular.

Winner of the event is the team which covers the greatest number of laps within the time set for the race. In the event of two or more teams finishing in the same lap, the victory goes, not to the winners of the final sprint, but to the team which has amassed the highest points score in the various sprints throughout the race. Besides the sixes, much shorter Madison events are also run and most countries hold a national Madison championship of around 50 kilometres or one hour.

Cyclo Cross

Apart from road-racing, time-trialling and track-racing, there is one further important branch of the sport: 'cyclo-cross' or cross-country racing which may be run on the same bunched-start principles as a road race or as a time-trial.

Courses usually involve a measure of running

Belgium's Rik I (Van Steenbergen) and Rik II (Van Looy) illustrate two phases of madison slinging. Van Looy grabs Van Steenbergen's seat-pad ready to throw him forward

Van Steenbergen repays the compliment, having completed his turn in the battle. Between them this pair won numerous six-day races and five world road titles

101

Cyclo-cross exponent Ian Jewell of Britain shoulders his bike for a steep uphill slog

on foot, with the bike carried across the shoulders, as well as riding on surfaces varying from cinders and grass to soft mud, vaulting over styles and gates, riding through streams and thickets and many other hazards.

A winter sport, cyclo-cross is great fun for spectator and competitor alike.

Learning to Race

The best school of all is, of course, racing itself. Supposing one has decided to take it up, how does one take the first steps? First off, you will need to join a reputable local club; your national federation (see page 106 for addresses) can help here.

British time-trialists need only be members of a club affiliated to the Road Time Trials Council, but British roadmen and 'trackies' must take out individual membership with the British Cycling Federation through their club. This membership automatically includes the issue of a domestic racing licence.

Riders in other countries must take out a racing licence with their appropriate UCI-affiliated federation. Those intending to race abroad will need an 'international licence' in addition.

Massed charge at the start of a cyclo-cross event. Snow and ice just add to the many hazards met in this thrilling brand of racing where spills are the norm

Your club will explain to you how to enter races. In most countries, this must be done several weeks in advance, but Belgian riders have the advantage of being able to enter races on the line. The French Federation very wisely requires a medical certificate before it grants a racing licence, and all who intend to race in France would be well advised to undergo a thorough health check — dental as well as medical — beforehand. A pre-season course of anti-tetanus injections is also advisable.

You need to be not just 'everyday fit' in order to race, but fit in an athletic sense, which means free of excess fatty tissues and with muscles carefully toned up for the extremes of exertion demanded. Training, like diet, is very much a personal affair and what is best for one man may not suit another but there are certain basic guidelines worth following. More books and magazine articles have been written on training than on any other cycling topic. It is as well to read as many of these as possible, and then to tailor the advice they contain to suit your own personal needs.

Never be over-ambitious in your training programme. Build up to peak form gradually, starting with short, gentle pre-season rides at around 15 mph, preferably in company, as

this breaks the monotony. Then slowly increase both distance and speed until you are doing rides of around 50 miles at 18 to 20 mph as the racing season gets under way.

Some riders train over vast distances—as much as 120 miles at a time even in mid-season, but most will get more benefit by fifty miles at near-racing speeds.

Riding out to races held within fifteen miles of home can be an advantage, as this is a good

Cornering techniques in a cycle speedway race are vastly different from those in more conventional forms of bicycle racing

103

way of loosening up.

Many riders today favour so-called interval training. This involves a short, sharp burst of effort followed by a winding down, and then another short burst. The favourite method is to sprint for 200 yards, slow down over the next 200 yards then sprint again. Twenty minutes of such effort should have you on your knees, but it certainly improves recovery rate after an effort—an important factor in racing—and many claim that it does as much good as three hours of ordinary training.

When training, always wrap up warmly and avoid hanging about in damp, sweaty clothing. It is better to tackle your training in a straight-off ride rather than stopping for refreshments *en route*, as this can lead to chills.

Learn to breathe properly, both off the bike and when riding, using the diaphragm to fill your lungs fully. But avoid taking in great gasps of chill air in wintry conditions.

You are embarking on one of the toughest, most demanding sports in the world but there is no need to live a Spartan existence. Racing should always be enjoyable, and so should your preparation for it. If it is pouring with rain then it is better to miss a night's road training; spend the time on indoor exercises or simply relaxing rather than embark on a miserable, sodden ride, and running the risk of picking up a cold. Preserve interests outside the sport; never become a narrow-minded fanatic. Fanaticism may improve your racing for a very short period, but it will soon make you lose interest, as well as turning you into a boring, self-centred person.

Hubert Opperman smashed road records in Australia and Britain, won the world's longest single-day race, Paris-Brest-Paris and competed in the Tour de France before 'retiring' to become an Australian cabinet minister

In 1899, the legendary Major Taylor became the only coloured man ever to have won a world cycling title

Heading the pack as always, Belgium's Eddy Merckx is now generally recognised as the greatest rider ever with a string of Tour de France, world championship and classic victories

Before Merckx, there was no denying Fausto Coppi's claim to the title of 'Campionissimo'—champion of champions. When the brilliant rider died in 1960, some 100,000 people attended his funeral and all Italy mourned

Bicycling organisations

British Cycling Federation
26 Park Crescent
London W1
The internationally-recognised controlling body for cycle racing in Great Britain, the BCF is affiliated to the Union Cycliste International (World governing body for cycle sport). Through a joint agreement, it leaves the administration of time-trial racing to the Road Time Trials Council, while itself governing road racing and track racing. The BCF also provides a touring service for members

British Cycling Bureau
Greater London House
Hampstead Road
London NW1
The British bicycle industry's information centre

AUSTRALIA

Amateur Cycling Association of Australia
34 Wardwell Road
Earlwood
Sydney, NSW
Controlling body for all amateur phases of the sport in Australia

British Professional Cycle Racing Association
W Mason
General Manager
Hebden Travel Lodge
Mill Lane
Hebden, near Skipton
Yorkshire
Fosters professional cycle racing in Britain under BCF rules

Australian Cycling Council
153 The Ringway
Cronulla, 2230
Sydney, NSW
Professional racing in Australia comes under the jurisdiction of this body

CANADA

British Cyclo Cross Association
5 Copstone Drive
Dorridge
Solihull
Warwickshire
Controlling body for cyclo-cross (cross-country) racing in Britain

Canadian Cycling Association
333 River Road
Vanier
Ontario
Cycle racing in Canada is the responsibility of the CCA

Road Time Trials Association
210 Devonshire Hill Lane
London N17 7NR
Time-trialling remains the most popular form of cycling competition in Britain and is controlled by the RTTC

Canadian Youth Hostels Association
268 First Avenue
Ottawa,
Ontario

Cyclists Touring Club
Cotterell House
69 Meadrow
Godalming, Surrey
Claimed to be the oldest national cycling organisation in the world, and a founder member of the Alliance Internationale de Tourisme (which now looks after motorists' interests as well), the CTC does valuable work in protecting cyclists' rights in Great Britain, as well as in providing an extremely comprehensive touring service, with maps, guides, recommended tours, meal and accommodation addresses. The CTC also organises guided tours in Britain and Europe and has District Associations which hold regular cycling and social events

Youth Hostels Association of England & Wales
Trevelyan House
8 St. Stephen's Way
St. Albans, Hertfordshire
Administers Youth Hostels throughout England and Wales, provides a tourist service and organises guided cycle tours

Scottish Youth Hostels Association
7 Bruntsfield Crescent
Edinburgh
Provides within the Scottish borders the same services as the YHA of England & Wales

IRELAND

Irish Cycling Federation
155 Shanliss Road
Shantry
Dublin 9
Eire
Cycle racing in the Irish Republic is organised by this federation also known as the CRE. Many races are, however, held under the rules of the National Cycling Association, which is not internationally recognised

Northern Ireland Cycling Federation
144 Princess Way
Portadown
County Armagh
Northern Ireland
Ulster's cycle racing sport is controlled by this

association, though the dissident NCA also operates north of the border

Cyclists Touring Club, Dublin District
Association
Secretary, C McNulty
16 Royse Road
Phibsboro
Dublin 7, Eire
Carries on the functions of the CTC in the Irish Republic

Cyclists Touring Club,
N. Ireland District Association
B Wheeler
19 Dunraven Park
Belfast BT 55LF
Northern Ireland
The CTC's Ulster branch

Irish Youth Hostels Association
39 Mountjoy Square
Dublin
Eire

Youth Hostels Association of Northern Ireland
28 Bedford Street
Belfast 2
Northern Ireland

NEW ZEALAND

New Zealand Cycling Association
P.O. Box 3104
Wellington
Internationally-recognised controlling body for cycling sport in New Zealand

USA

Amateur Bicycle League of America
4233, 205th Street
Bayside
Long Island
New York
Amateur cycle racing within the USA is controlled by the ABL which is affiliated to the UCI and the US Olympic Committee and is associated with the Amateur Athletic Union of the US

Reading list

Professional Racing Organisation of America
310 Olly Street
Denver 80220
Colorado
*Governing body of professional bicycle racing in the
USA*

American Youth Hostels Inc.
20 West 17th Street
New York
NY 10011
*As a member of the International Youth Hostels
Federation, the AYH administers youth hostels
throughout the USA, provides a touring information
service and sells cycle touring equipment to members.
Cycle tours in the US and abroad are organised by
the AYH*

Bicycle Institute of America
122 East 42nd Street
New York
NY 10017
*Sponsored by the American cycle industry, the BIA
provides booklets and other information on all forms
of cycling activity from campaigning for special
bike-only routes to organising cycling clubs and
racing and touring events*

League of American Wheelmen Inc.
5118 Foster Avenue
Chicago
Illinois 60630
*The pioneer American cycling body, the LAW
promotes national and local touring events and seeks
to encourage the cycling pastime and protect its
interests*

International Bicycle Touring Society
846 Prospect Street
La Jolla
California 92037
*Headed by tourist-extraordinary Dr. Clifford Graves,
this body promotes the famous Huff'n' Puff tours in
the USA and abroad, which attract enthusiasts
ranging from prominent business people, airline
pilots and professional men to manual workers and
housewives*

Magazines

'Bicycling!'
H. M. Leete & Co.
15 Sir Francis Drake Blvd.
East Greenbrae
California 94904
(monthly)
*'Bicycling!' covers every sphere of cycling activity for
the American enthusiast, with news and feature
coverage of touring, racing, maintenance and
equipment*

'Cycling'
161–166 Fleet Street
London EC4
(weekly)
*Established in 1891, 'Cycling' is the world's oldest
publication in this field and, although it is primarily
aimed at cycle-racing followers, it also includes
features on touring and trade news*

'International Cycle Sport'
Kennedy Bros. Publishing Ltd.
St. John Street
Silsden
near Keighley
Yorkshire
(monthly)
*Well produced, with extensive use of colour
photographs, ICS is purely a racing publication and
gives excellent coverage of the sport in Great Britain
and Europe. A special American edition is
obtainable from the magazine's US office at 3570
Warrensville Center Road, Shaker Heights,
Ohio 44122*

'L'Equipe Cyclisme'
10 Faubourg Montmartre
Paris 9e
France
(monthly)
*Superb photographic reportage of the top
Continental races plus articles in French on racing,
training and preparation*

'Miroir du Cyclisme'
10 Rue des Pyramides
Paris 1e
France
(*monthly*)
Even if he has no command of French, this magazine holds much of interest for the racing enthusiast since photo reporting predominates. The results of each month's top continental races are carried. Special colour editions are produced during the Tour de France

'Le Cycliste'
18 Rue du Commandeur
Paris 14e
France
(*monthly*)
Much can be learned by the touring enthusiast from the beautiful technical illustrations in this extremely detailed publication

'L'Equipe'
10 Faubourg Montmartre
Paris 1e
France
(*weekly*)
The French daily sporting paper, 'l'Equipe' carries extensive cycling coverage, particularly during the Tour de France, of which the paper is the main sponsor

'Cycle Touring'
Cotterell House
69 Meadrow
Godalming
Surrey
(*monthly*)
Free to members of the Cyclists Touring Club, 'Cycle Touring' is packed with informative articles and illustrations. Non-members may obtain this publication by annual subscription

'Bike World'
2562 Middlefield Road
Mountain View
California 94040
(*monthly*)
An informative monthly publication covering racing, touring and technical matters in both text and well-reproduced photographs and drawings

Books

The Bicycle, its Care and Maintenance
Iliffe Books Ltd.
London 1961
A very useful handbook

Bicycling
by Ruth and Ray Benedict
A S Barnes & Co.
New York 1944
A dated but worthwhile guide to cycling's pleasures

Bikes and Riders
by James Wagenvoord
Van Nostrand Reinhold Co.
New York 1972
A fine book which, besides giving an account of early cycling history, has chapters which evoke the atmosphere of present-day cycling in its varied guises. Extremely well written and illustrated

The Complete Book of Bicycling
by Eugene A Sloane
Trident Press
New York 1970
One of the most detailed books yet published on the sport and pastime of cycling, including a lengthy repair and maintenance section. Many illustrations. Written from an American point-of-view

Continental Cycle Racing
by N G Henderson
Pelham Books
London 1970
The history and detailed results of the major Continental tours and one-day classics

Cycling Book of Maintenance
Temple Press Books
London 1961
Useful tips, especially for the novice

Cycling Crazy
by Charles Messenger
Pelham Books
London 1970
One of a series of extremely evocative books written by this former British team manager recalling incidents from three decades of racing in Britain and abroad (also Conquer the World Pelham Books 1970)

Cycling Handbook
by A L Pullen
Sir Isaac Pitman & Sons Ltd.
London 1960
Now badly in need of revision, this book none the less includes much information of value on all aspects of cycling

Cycling in the Sixties
by David Saunders
Pelham Books
London 1971
Personal memories of a decade of cycling sport from one of Britain's leading cycling journalists and TV commentators

Cycling is my life
by Tom Simpson
Stanley Paul
London 1966
The autobiography of Tom Simpson, Britain's world champion cyclist who died tragically in the 1967 Tour de France

Cycling Manual
by R John Way
Temple Press Books Ltd.
London 1967
Regularly up-dated editions of this publication give a fairly complete guide to cycling, and include fine coverage of the technical and maintenance side of things

Cycling Year Book
by N G Henderson
Pelham Books
London
(annually)
An analysis of the year's racing in Britain and on the continent of Europe

Full Tilt: Ireland to India by Bicycle
by Dervla Murphy
E P Dutton & Co Inc
New York 1965
Delightfully-written account of a young Irish woman's adventurous cycling journey from her homeland to India

Teach Yourself Cycling
by Reg Shaw
English Universities Press
London 1963
Exactly what the title says

Tour de France
by Peter Clifford
Stanley Paul
London 1965
The detailed history of the Tour de France from its inception in 1903, including detailed results and analysis

The Turned Down Bar
by Nancy Neiman
Dorance & Co.
Philadelphia 1964
The story of one of America's finest lady champions of the post-war era

What will you do, Jim?
by Ralph Hurne
Michael Joseph
London 1966
A perceptively-written novel on the career of a professional racing cyclist. This book provides an insight into what the tough world of top-flight cycling competition is like

The series of illustrated booklets produced by 'International Cycle Sport' (see magazine addresses) are useful. They include *Legends of Cycling, Uncrowned Kings of Cycling, Reg Harris, Louison Bobet* and *Cycle Racing Tactics*, all by the author of the present book, and *Yellow Jersey, Maître Jacques—the Jacques Anquetil Story, Six of the Best, Eddy Merckx, Rainbow Jersey, World Champions I Have Known* and *The Emperor—the Rik Van Looy Story*, written by various top-flight cycling authorities.
Produced annually by leading cycling journalist René Jacobs, the Belgian publication 'Vélo', René Jacobs, c/o 'Les Sports', Bruxelles, Belgium, is invaluable, being composed entirely of detailed results of the year's racing, both professional and amateur, together with results, tables of all the top continental races back to their inception.